FOOTBALL FOR THE BRAVE

By John Cartwright

PUBLISHED BY

m-press
(MEDIA) LIMITED

FOOTBALL FOR THE BRAVE

TEXT ©John Cartwright

Further copies of this book may be ordered by visiting the Publishers website
www.calmproductions.com
or by telephoning our mail order hotline 0845 4082606

Unit 4, Ashton Gate, Ashton Road, Harold Hill, Romford, Essex. RM3 8UF

Tel: 01708 379777 Fax: 01708 379979
email: mpa@mpressltd.com

FORWARD

By **Roy Hodgson – Manager of Fulham FC**.

John Cartwright has produced a thoughtful book which thoroughly differs from most books of this "genre". After a lifetime in football spent championing the need for more skillful players and better coaching to develop those individuals, John Cartwright has given us a book which pulls no punches. The book will not only provoke a lot of thought, and maybe even debate, but be one that can inspire coaches to follow his example and to dedicate the time and effort it takes to produce highly skilled footballer's who are capable of adapting to the needs of the modern game.

Truly a "brave" effort and really well done, so I therefore hope the book reaches the audience it deserves.

To my wife Naomi,
for all her support and patience

Acknowledgments

To Roy Hodgson for writing the Forward to this book; Ken Goldman for his great assistance with the script; Cliff Moulder for his work on the publication side; and Roger Wilkinson, Ryan McKnight and Teddy Moen for their encouragement and support.

Author's Comments

This is not the usual football coaching book or manual. It does not contain text supporting illustrations or various drills or practices.

I have attempted to draw the reader's attention to the important aspects related to the playing and coaching of the game and have used famous players, past and present as examples.

I have emphasised throughout the book the importance of individual skill in the game. I refute the 'easily digestible' belief that 'football is a team game' and offer an alternative belief that 'football is a game for individuals to combine when necessary'.

I have targeted the decline of individual skill and quality in the British game and have commented on the reasons for this decline and what could be done to improve the situation.

In particular, I have tried to underline the importance of mental bravery in attempting skillful performance and the need to resist simplicity as a single option offered by too many coaches to our young players.

John Cartwright

Introduction

I remember it as if it was yesterday. It was the summer of 1958 and I had watched the World Cup on television from Sweden.

It was the first time I had watched Brazil play and my eyes could not absorb enough of their talent. For me, it was a tall, black player who distinguished himself above everyone else – Pelé included – the player's name was Didi.

This player moved effortlessly over the ground and the ball seemed to obey his every touch, displaying guile and skill that was a joy to behold.

This was how I knew the game should be played; skillfully and athletically. There was a rhythm in the way Brazil played the game; there was harmony in the way they combined, and their individualism was pure music!

Later that same year, I was then 17, and had just signed my first professional contract at West Ham United. The team Manager decided he wanted a practice match between the first team and reserves at the main Stadium, Upton Park, on a Tuesday morning. I was in the reserves but thrilled to be playing against the senior pros, especially in the main stadium.

It all happened so simply. I received a throw-in near the half way line; instead of playing the ball back to the thrower, I 'dummied' and allowed the ball to roll on past me. From there I ran forward with the ball beating another defender. Just outside the penalty area I combined with a team-mate with a 'wall-pass' and hit his return into the top of the goal from about 20 yards – GOAL! Yes a real classic!

As I walked back to the centre circle, Ted Fenton, the Manager, who had been watching from the directors box, stood up and, with the aid of an electric megaphone called out my name; 'CARTWRIGHT, WHY DON'T YOU DO IT SIMPLE? EVERYONE ELSE CARRY ON AS NORMAL, CARTWRIGHT, YOU PLAY TWO TOUCH!'

I was being told to be ordinary! For me the 'music of the game' died.

It is my belief that individual skill is the core of good football performance. From the very start of my involvement with coaching I was determined to champion the skillful player. I promised myself never to 'kill the music' for anyone who worked with me as a coach or a player.

I trust I have been brave and honest enough to fulfil that promise.

FOOTBALL FOR THE BRAVE

CONTENTS

CHAPTER  # HOPE OR DESPAIR

'The sweat you lose whilst training saves the blood in war'
Mao Tse-Tung

Without a vision to aspire to, life becomes a 'fog' of indecision, false starts, frustration and failure.

Currently, our football, throughout the UK, lacks the vision of how we should play the game; therefore we fail!

Without a vision, a way forward is uncertain and any planning is likely to be fragmented and largely under-productive.

In these islands too much of our football is played in an expectation of hope not certainty'. The essential discussions at the top to determine the content of a suitable national playing style has not been considered necessary. This has produced a disconnected and shambolic approach in both development and playing incurring time wastage and financial loss.

How can coaches be taught and players produced to play without first establishing a suitable national playing style? The content of this game style should be based upon both national characteristics and the anticipated requirements of the World Game over, say a projected period of 25 years. Club football could use this national game style 'template' and adapt it accordingly to their individual requirements.

At present, in our desperation to achieve success in our 'blind' approach, we lurch from one failure to another with often more attention focused on physical preparation and team formations than on teaching how to play the game.

A national playing style 'template' would allow the building blocks for progress to be clearly set out. Important foundations could be prioritised and effected to provide the game with the strong supports it needs to eliminate mistakes and create and maintain success at club and international levels.

An example of our disorganised approach is obvious when it comes to skills for the game. We know the game should include individual skills but we don't produce it so we import it – not a healthy prospect for our football future!

The shortages of 'home grown' talent has increased costs in transfer fees and salaries, especially by use of agents. Combined with these, the increased cost of ground improvements has left many clubs in desperate financial difficulties.

When cut-backs occur they usually hit the most vulnerable – the development section – resulting in even less opportunities for young players to establish themselves!

Because Association Football is such a fantastic product world wide, business has been keen to involve itself deeply into the game. Big companies invest large amounts of money; none more so than TV companies. Advertising based on viewing figures propels money into the game. Investment on this scale demands immediate results to appease shareholders; therefore, the established player is preferred over younger talent.

The effects of incompetent leadership with no vision; no long term planning and financial naivity have produced incredible mistakes by the English FA. In their confused state they have allowed powerful 'competitors' to invade their territory. These rival camps have evolved and flourished. It will be interesting to see the results of these continuing intrusions in the future!

It might well be asked, how much longer our footballing integrity can be maintained when so much 'hype' affirming mediocrity is heaped upon the game. In the downward spiral of British football, ordinary is too often referred to as great! Honest opinions and not 'hyped' deceit must regain a foothold in the game. Leadership must establish a better developmental framework and exorcise the 'hyped' camouflaging of average for a more honest appreciation of the true skillful qualities needed in the game.

For well over half a century our FA have been responsible for coaching and development standards. Why, after all this time, have their methods failed to produce the necessary quality in 'home grown' coaching and playing talent? Answer – Lack of vision and poor planning.

In the past, football did not have the extensive coaching and development networks seen today. Kids played in the streets, in school playgrounds and on any available flat waste ground. Games included as many as wanted to play, with anything resembling a ball, in usually small, congested areas. Refereeing was done amongst themselves with any disputes quickly dealt with – arguments reduced playing time and nothing was more important then playing! When friends were unavailable to play you kicked a ball against a wall, juggled with it, or dribbled around bricks – the ball was touched thousands of times each week with the result that the ball became a friend and not a bouncing foe.

In conjunction with ball skills came decision-making. Football decisions were gained in realistic situations that were easily transferable into the more elaborate atmosphere of competitive match play.

The products of street 'practice/play' football were still just about evident in our senior game into the mid-1970s and because of the unstructured development process these players had experienced their skill levels for the game were of a high level but their game understanding was weak.

The great strides made economically and socially that have taken place throughout this country since the 1960s have also brought about big changes in the methods for producing footballer's.

The car; TV; rebuilding etc have driven kids from their old 'practice/play' areas and led to the introduction of more organised football development methods. The structured presentation of organised coaching for kids has changed the type of player produced for the game dramatically.

Previously, players learnt to play the game in 'chaos-type' situations but with the introduction of coaching, styled on formal academic teaching method, players have become less individualistic and more team-orientated.

footballer's need to be taught the game properly. I do not believe that players are 'born footballers'. Some may have better opportunities from a younger age, but generally good guidance of good potential will produce exciting talent.

Unfortunately, without the benefit of visionary planning in the development of our young players, a 'poisonous cocktail' of negative influences has derailed young player development. Parents, teachers, coaching courses, competitive football, media hype, each has caused an unmistakable but ever-increasing decrease in the number of naturally skillful 'home-grown' players for our game.

A 'winning at all costs' attitude infects all levels of the game. 'Winning Methods', lacking skillful performance can be seen in junior games through to international football at senior level. In the frenzy to win, the instinctive qualities required for high-level performance have been discarded. A Catch-22 situation ferments in the coaching/playing cauldron; poor coach education methods; produces poor coaches; who produce poor players; who play poor quality football; to win poor quality matches.

Greatness is an unachievable level for coaches and players brought through the development and playing methods currently preferred by the leaders of football education in this country.

A pre-occupation with 'tidy practice' and over organisation has strangled realism, spontaneity and individualism amongst our coaches and players. The importance of decision-making on time and space in both practising and playing has been largely ignored by the coaching fraternity. Too much emphasis has been given to 'choreographed' and 'regimented' practice to produce technical ability. We have not understood that football is not played with technique but with skill. Skill demands decisions on time and space as they affect both the attacking and defending situations of the game. Our coaching methods have not produced ideas or methods for practices in which kids can develop skills realistically for easy transfer into competitive match-play.

At coaching courses held throughout this country, paperwork not practice dominates the coaching programmes. So much time is assigned to insignificant detail one often wonders why? Perhaps, the answer is that the teachers of the game are more comfortable in classroom situations with paper, projectors and computers than outside with practice sessions on real grass or artificial surfaces!

Too many coaches are happier talking than doing. The proportion of doing to listening must increase substantially if our young players are to attain the skills to play the game.

Football needs kids to do what comes naturally to kids – play football ! What coaching must provide is a modern approach that will allow realistic understanding and development to occur whilst play/practice is in progress.

A new visionary approach followed by forward planning is essential if our game is to survive. Unless those in charge are prepared to discard the 'mantle of mediocrity' firmly attached to our game and lift ideas and expectations upwards, we are in for a very uncertain and frustrating footballing future.

CHAPTER

SKILL – THE GAME'S IMPORTANT CORE

My definition of skill is…

'The learned ability to bring about pre-determined results with maximum certainty, according to time and space limitations and with minimum outlay of effort.'

But a definition of skill more suitable for the game of football played in this country could be…

'Skill is a rote learned ability to achieve a pre-determined result with simple outcomes and with no space/time awareness, but with maximum outlay of effort.'

People ask me, 'Can we win the World Cup again?'
My reply is not meant to dodge the question, it is, 'Well, we're difficult to beat'.
But really, is being difficult to beat enough? Surely the winners of such a prestigious trophy needs to have more than the qualities of low order Boxers.

It is true, however, that our competitive instincts make us formidable opponents… nobody enjoys playing against British teams, we're the 'terriers' of football. However, if we are to draw an analogy from the animal kingdom it should be the cheetah, not wild dogs we must try to emulate, for the cheetah hunts cunningly with speed and skill!

Future skills acquisition time must place more emphasis on transference into competitive match-play. This type of practice with young players should dominate the formative years of development. With this in mind, the importance placed on coaching methodology and on the coaches working with the game's future players is enormous. Good coaching should instill good habits from an early age or else mere damage limitation follows. 'Papering over the cracks' best describes so much of the present situation in coaching terms with our senior players who have progressed through our development programmes.

The stature of the talented coach should not be under-estimated. The position demands not only a deep understanding of the game but bravery to enforce beliefs and to emphasise the importance of individual development above team play throughout the early development years.

Team-play, in which the natural competitive instincts of children and their parents as well as their coaches to win football matches must not be discarded, but competitive match-play must be introduced more cleverly and more carefully, with gradual competitive stages that lead up to the full game.

Our young players must be allowed to play competitively according to the level and type of practice they are working on. The competitive match, when played, should, at all levels, reflect the type of work being done at the time. What's the sense of practising junior levels of work and then throwing the young players into scaled-down versions of the full game. The two aspects; practice, followed by competitive match, should complement, not oppose each other.

There is an urgent need for our National Association to develop a new junior competitive game. Instead of 'copy-catting' the senior game, our young players from six to the age of 11 should be playing a junior game that offers winning and losing but in a carefully structured way that incorporates the work in progress at the time at each age level.

Our coach education methods tend to follow a classroom approach, whereby necessity, there is a need for control; group organisation and formal structure. This isn't surprising as schoolteachers have been in control of our coaching since the early 1950s. Our football should not be represented by dull academic conformity. The game is better aligned with showbusiness where, fantasy, thrills, supporting acts and individual star quality all combine together. Creativity evolves from organised 'chaos-type learning' situations, not controlled conformity. Our coaching methods have set targets to produce the 'chorus line' not the leading players of the show!

Simplistic football decisions must be an option for players to use, not a necessity! All our early development planning should relate to the production of individual excellence that is taught to combine within a team structure; not mediocrity that must rely solely on the team to survive!

Skill is pressurised technique. If it is skill the competitive game examines, surely, players should develop skills in pressurised practices suitably arranged for ages and levels of work. I find it hard to understand how 'drill routines' supposed to improve skill quality can be used so much when they offer no considerations or decisions on time and space to players.

Football skill is about effective performance in the limited space and time provided by competition. For so many youngsters, technical competence does not transfer into competitive play. A practice must offer realism to the participant... practice how you play! Time and space decisions form a very large part of our every-day life-styles. Competitive football makes the same demands on players. The astute coach must formulate skill practices that will provide realistic and regular opportunities for time and space decision making to occur continuously. Unrealistic practice is time spent wastefully !

In order to cover skill deficiencies, speed and strength have become increasingly prominent in our game. Although both of these athletic qualities are vitally important for player and team they should complement 'core skill'. Lack of individuals who are comfortable on the ball in all playing areas has brought about a reduction in tactical options in our game. Rigid conformity to team shape is the result.

'Half players (all physical but short of skill, or all skill but no physical presence) litter our game This 'production line' of enforced mediocrity requires a 'patchwork' team selection to spread the thinly available talent. The playing styles resulting from such undistinguished talent has made the playing of our game; unimaginative; straight-lined in approach and leads too often to 'confrontational battles'.

Lack of skill has increased the anxiety and tension in the game. Coaches, players, directors and supporters involved at the senior end of the game as well as those attached to the lower levels are all sitting on edge of their seats, praying for the right result... a winning one! Little confidence is shown for players who have skill but lack a physical presence; too often the 'athletic bruiser' is preferred... even at the very junior levels of our game... winning is everything! In order that conformity is retained, simplistic football is demanded. Our game is riddled with cowardly attitudes that suggest attractive football can't be successful football!

Like most things in life, striking a balance generally proves the best approach to follow for sustained success. It must be recognised that, irrespective of whatever way the game is played, it requires high skill levels to play it well. No 'easy gimmick' playing method can succeed without the involvement of skillful individuals. It is the skill that is introduced into the game that 'puts the icing on the cake' and makes the game unpredictable and exciting to watch.

Playing styles with limited options and simplistic football methods are all a consequence of the poor development of players during the 'Golden Years of Skill Learning' (5-14). Acquiring the habits of 'instinctive play' can only be achieved by practising in realistic, instinct-forming situations. The ability to 'Play in the Future' (have instinctive awareness) can only develop through a continuous exposure to realistic practice methods. In the heat of competitive play, speed of thought and reaction must provide players with a 'protective shield' against surprise. Slow reacting players have no chance in the hurley-burley of today's football.

Realistic practice stimulates the imaginative qualities required for skillful play. Structured learning methods have 'dulled' the minds and actions of our players. The need for a skill to be performed must first be 'seen' in the mind of the player before it can be transferred into physical movement. The production of these 'pictures' and the speed to reproduce them into actions must be practiced realistically in varying circumstances throughout the whole of the development years – and continued throughout the senior time in the game.

If we want imaginative, quick-thinking, skillful players then we must provide the means to produce them. We have been following our present production path for over 50 years with little or no success. Our National Association, in whose hands coach education rests, has great difficulty, due to its size and financial commitment to outdated coaching methods, to make the significant changes required. Whilst they stutter and stumble from one crisis to another, all of our domestic leagues need foreign 'imports' to bolster skill deficiencies; and our game becomes more aggressive and ill-tempered as our physical style 'bumps up' against foreign skill.

We've seen how 'brave' our lads are for decades – blood streaming from wounds; injured players staying on in the 'fight'; or playing with their 'backs to the wall' after a team-mate's red-card dismissals. All very well but if it was just physical bravery alone I wanted to watch I can put the TV on each night and watch this type of bravery in a boxing ring. No, it's braver to encourage better quality football that needs to be highlighted and offered. The hiding behind so-called 'bravery' to engender the 'feel sorry for us ' factor has run its course – sympathy is running short for our well-paid but under-achieving players.

Unless we take a very long and honest look at what's happening in our game and make some drastic decisions we will continue our 'slide' down football's slippery slope and gross sub-standard performances will continue to represent greatness for us.

CHAPTER

FOOTBALL IS A SIDEWAYS GAME

'Play on the half-turn in both attacking and defensive situations"

Being prepared for any eventuality seems only common sense. In all areas of daily life we take careful note of any situation in which we become involved.

In places or situations we're not familiar with we take special care to look more keenly about us – even over our shoulder – we are prepared for the unexpected! Most sports are played from a sideways position; this makes the movement to strike easier as well as to be well positioned to see as much of the pitch and surrounding area as possible. Sport requires performers to adjust their body positioning according to the actions required for quick, accurate responses.

Football in particular is a game that should be played on the half turn (shoulders diagonally set across the field – not straight across it!)

Manufacturing correct body positions opens up more visual aspects of the game to the player. In football, where challenges can come from any direction; being surprised by a quick tackle or a subtle off the ball run by an opponent is extremely unlikely to catch the well-positioned player unaware. Playing the game of football is not about being surprised or unaware; it's about knowing! Early visual clues allow quick and accurate decisions to be made – all the time.

Playing 'blind' (poor body positioning) hinders performance to the extent that luck not judgement affects the result. Great players are 'tuned-in' all the time in both attacking and defending situations. Gaining an advantage over them is difficult. Their body positioning eliminates surprises and provides them with distinct advantages. There is no gambling on their part and decisions are made on visual evidence not blind hope.

There have been so many aspiring young footballer's that have shown high levels of technical quality on the training ground but, unfortunately, fail in competitive match play. Regardless of their technical quality they become frustrated by their inability to satisfy the skill requirements of the game. Poor practice methods that exclude realism and waste so much of the development time lie at the base of so many failing to reach the heights in the game.

Playing for the 'Dog and Duck' or for a senior professional club could be the difference of half a metre. A body adjustment (half turn) positioning by a player can be the difference between failure or success. In all areas of the field a half turned shape is vital for players to visually gather information and use it quickly and effectively.

When defending: players must note visually and mentally…

- The position of the ball
- His / her positioning relating to covering or marking
- The movement and positioning of team-mates and opponents
- Calculating the options

When attacking: players must have awareness of:

- Where is the ball?
- Where are the marking / covering opponents?
- Where are the spaces?
- Where are my supporting players?
- Can I hold the ball, turn, pass or run with it?
- Do I need to pass first time?

All this information must be recognised first before answers can be given. None of this information can be correctly read or analysed from 'blind' positioning. In success terms it could mean owning a Rolls-Royce or a Morris Minor car!

Some Coaches say: 'Think and grow rich.' I say: 'See and be rich – the view is up to you!'

From the earliest years practice must emphasise the importance of the half-turned shape. It must become a habit, a platform from which high performance can be launched. When we watch great players involved in fierce competitive situations produce skills that thrill us, we must remember the skills and decisions they make have been computed in their brain from visual signals. Top players must produce fast decisions and actions to overcome high quality defenders who are equally capable of reducing the effectiveness of opponents. Sound judgement, not 'lady luck' forms the basis of the great players' game. A great performance is only 'half a metre away' – (half turn)!

As already mentioned in Chapter Two, young players should be developed through a series of carefully progressed small area practices in order to familiarise themselves with the essential decision making process, demanded by time and space restrictions. By learning to play on the half turn in realistic, competitive practices, good habits that will last a lifetime can be established.

Player to Watch: Dennis Bergkamp, Arsenal and Holland

We think of the game in Britain as fast, tough and tight. The importation of skillful overseas players into our Premier League caused interest in their ability to cope with the high-pressured intensity of our 'blue ribbon' domestic league.

Bergkamp, after his arrival at Arsenal FC, took a little time to settle in. His early games were often disappointing as he sought to find a balance between the slower, more skillful European game style he had been brought up on and played successfully in, and the faster more direct method used here.

However, before too long Bergkamp was 'leading the orchestra'.

He developed an ability to 'sink' slightly deeper in a revised attacking role and combined with his ability to play on the half turn his performances improved.

Arsenal FC enjoyed considerable success inspired by Bergkamp's inspired performances over the years. His obvious football talents are not easily suppressed by close marking defenders. By his ability to adjust his body shape (half-turn) and find spaces that defenders found hard to fill, he provided the forward 'link' so important in advanced attacking areas. His superb awareness and subsequent fast decisions provided flowing attacking play and goals for 'the Gunners' as well as for Holland.

Bergkamp learned his football 'trade' in Holland and the hours spent mastering the 'football business' were obviously well spent. Every touch-pass-movement we observe him perform under the severest pressure of top-flight football was forged and honed on the practice areas throughout all his junior and senior years.

No aspect of practice was more important for him than that which emphasised good body positioning (half-turn) for both attacking and defending situations. It has enabled him to receive the adulation of the football public only reserved for truly great players.

Perhaps a quote from his then Arsenal Manager, Bruce Rioch, sums up Bergkamp's qualities to the full: 'Dennis understands everything, but the Dutch aren't brought up to say very much. The coaches over there ask them to use their eyes, not their mouths. Rather than talk about it, he visualises in his mind how he wants to perform.'

Player to Watch: Paolo Maldini, AC Milan, Italy

We more often give attacking players as examples of qualities on the ball and artful subtlety in the playing of the game but defenders are also expected to provide skills and movement. Like any other player, defenders as already mentioned, need to position themselves correctly to allow them to defend well and to follow this with successful attacking play.

Maldini, as a defender is very rarely extended. His use of the 'jockeying' position (half-turn) provides him with: guiding, marking, tackling and sprinting options against opposing players. His body shape deprives attackers of

the opportunities to 'sneak' into positions from which they can make runs behind or across him, whilst it also allows him to see both the ball and the player he is marking. Without preparing to defend by 'shaping up' properly, good defensive play is impossible.

Maldini is yet another of those players who are 'convertible'.

His football talent is immense and his success lies in his ability to put himself in the right position at the right time.

Whoever explained, taught or encouraged Maldini to make playing on the half-turn a football habit played a significant role in producing one of today's football greats.

Player to Watch: Paul Gascoigne Spurs, Lazio, Rangers, England

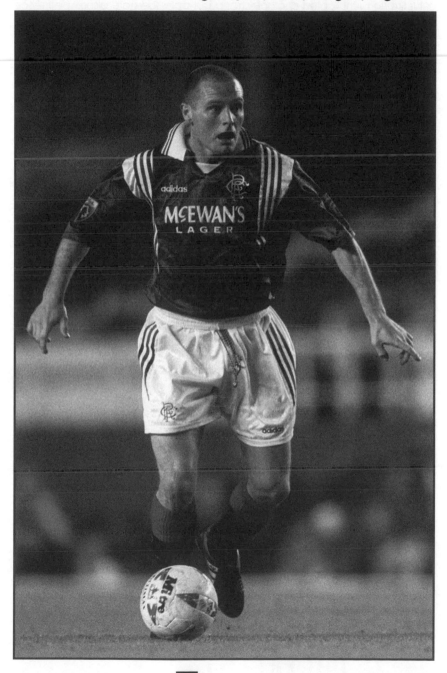

Much has been written about Gazza's antics on and off the field. In both areas of his life his complicated character has been a positive and negative influence on his performances. However, whenever Gascoigne's talent emerged he displayed periods of artistry and imagination that few others of his day came near to copying.

It was not generally recognised that he possessed a strong physique and he used this strength to resist the contact his type of performance would receive from rugged, tight marking opponents.

Gascoigne received and held the ball up well because he was prepared to take the ball on the half turn and, using his strength and skill he generated time and space to produce his brand of magic with the ball. He should be applauded as a player who, despite the oppressive football culture of our game, would not settle for mediocrity but sought higher, more skillful football objectives.

CHAPTER

4

BE CONFIDENT PLAYING IN TIGHT AREAS

What a joy it is to observe a real craftsman at work. Irrespective of the type of trade, it is a privilege to see difficult jobs performed with technical dexterity, understanding and speed.

However, football, unlike most trades, is not an unopposed technical process; it is actively competitive requiring skills to 'produce the goods'.

Therefore, from their earliest involvement with the game, all young players should be developed to be comfortable and assured when in possession of the ball and under pressure from opposing players.

The game of football involves players moving the ball and themselves around the field of play; a player or players in one area of the field interlinking with a player or players in another part of the field. It follows that players should practice what the game demands of them – become confident and skillful playing in small areas and able to link effectively from area to area.

Working in progressively tight, competitive areas during practice, increases the development of acute football decisions in players as they continue through their learning process. To make more correct decisions than incorrect ones will distinguish the better from the lesser player.

'Animal-like' awareness can be developed to distinguish the various 'signals' players receive to assist them in selecting an appropriate skill and the speed required to perform it effectively. Realistic 'signals' can only be obtained through realistic practice. 'Signals' that lead to decisions in the game provide the split-seconds and fractions of centimetres (time and space) reactions by players and must be part of everyday practice.

Realistic practices in grids or groups develops the necessary qualities required by players for the competitive game. Coaches must promote individual creativity in these sorts of practices for it has become a scarce ability in our game. Players who can play with imagination whilst under pressure radiate the potential of greatness.

Previously, Pelé, Maradona and now Ronaldinho exhibit supreme composure in pressurised situations at the highest level. They exemplify how great players adapt their skills quickly to suit all circumstances and provide answers to seemingly impossible questions set them in games.

These players and many more throughout the world of football, developed their instinctive awareness and skillful response in their junior years of playing in the various streets across the globe, with small balls and limited play areas during thousands of hours practice-playing the game.

In countries where this type of development process has largely disappeared, it has been replaced by a coaching culture more interested in organisation of practice than the realistic teaching of the game. There has been a significant over-use of unopposed 'drill' practices combined with an explosion in the use of 11 vs 11 match play at too early an age. This is not the way to produce individualism and high quality players. The combination of these drill practices and team match-play reduces 'signal' awareness, decisions and touches of the ball – mediocrity is made not greatness!

A matador, facing a raging bull, must make instantaneous decisions. With fear, his constant companion, the matador must produce a careful, skillful, fast and entertaining performance in the limited space of the bullring where the smallest mistake on his part can result in injury or death.

It should be stressed to coaches that it is their job to produce players for 'football's cauldrons'. The players that they produce must have the ability to perform to equally high standards in similar tense and pressurised circumstances – although mistakes here are not punishable by death!

Player to Watch: Pelé, Brazil
Pelé was an ordinary kid who was brought up in a poor area of Brazil. Football was 'king' and was played anywhere football could be played. These areas were

usually untidy, uneven surfaces and poverty meant the ball was small. Each of these factors made control of the ball difficult. Combined with these problems the large numbers of youngsters who wanted to play could also be a decisive factor.

The good players developed the ability to keep the ball in the congestion and chaos around them. Pelé became an expert in 'seeing' ways through and adapted and modified his skills to suit the difficult playing situations that required split-second decisions to be made as well as delicate touch on the ball.

It was only a step up to senior football for Pelé and those who developed in a similar fashion. It must have seemed a luxury to play on good surfaces with so much space. The game was relatively easy for him at this level and he used the skills and instincts he had learned at home on the football fields all around the world.

The close attention of 'raging bull' defenders brought no fear to Pelé. Like a master matador he skilled his way through a fabulous career that brought credit to him and joy to all who watched him play – what he himself described as 'The Beautiful Game'.

Player to Watch: Maradona, Argentina

For Maradona, one could simply rewrite Pelé's tribute again. It is important to note that both of these fabulous players emerged onto the world scene from similar developmental backgrounds. Those circumstances created their individualistic qualities that they reproduced in football stadia all over the football world.

Maradona was explosive in a game. He was able to provide magic in an instant. He had a remarkable ability to play using only his left foot. He had the 'instinctive eye' to plot a course through the tightest of defences. He saw the gaps and used the space and time available to exploit situations and score goals or provide assists for others throughout his career.

I first saw Maradona on a video. He was part of an Argentinean under 20s team playing in a world youth tournament in Australia. I thought the film was faulty and was running too fast. Maradona seemed to skip quickly and effortlessly past defenders.

He became famous for the individual skill he provided to a game. None more so than his well-remembered individual effort against England In the 1986 Mexico World Cup.

Maradona was a product of the street, an individual who played the way he had always played the game.

Player to Watch: Ronaldinho, Brazil

Ronaldinho is yet another wonderful player to come from Brazil.

The instinctive qualities of so many wonderful players from this part of the world are again represented through the outstanding performances of Ronaldinho.

He has those mystical qualities of the truly great player: the ability to be unpredictable and be able to adapt to a variety of situations with an immediacy that is truly amazing.

Once again the qualities were created amongst the chaos of street football. Imagination and invention are at the very heart of Ronaldinho's game. His trickery and deftness of movement create goals for himself and others.

Crowds adore his cleverness and ability to unlock any opposing defence or beat the most resolute of marking players. He has a 'foxy eye' for situations that was developed from his young playing days. It sometimes seems he can 'see through the back of his head' when he disguises his passes so cunningly!

He is also 'fleet of foot' not just in terms of his running speed but his flexibility of movement and his touch on the ball bemuses and tantalises defenders especially with his clever 'dummy' plays on the ball.

Like all tricky great players he is capable of winning games from the most unlikely of situations. He's done it so often in the past and, without doubt, will continue to do so in the future.

CHAPTER

RUN WITH BALL IN A POSITIVE MANNER AT EVERY OPPORTUNITY

'Don't run with the ball! Pass it! Give it easy! Who do you think you are, Ronaldinho?'

How often have we heard those damning words or similar expletives screamed at young players? All too often, talent, in need of encouragement and guidance, receives abuse and ridicule.

To satisfy the 'safety first' mentality within our game, a lesser, uninspiring imitation of football quality is preferred. Instead of the high ground of excellence being sought, the level ground of mediocrity is the only standard visualised as achievable for our young talent.

Hardly anyone stays on the ball anymore. From top to bottom our game does not possess players capable of tantalising opponents or make penetrative runs through defensive 'barriers'. Nobody except our foreign 'imports' who have a different outlook / culture on the way the game should be played.

Can anyone imagine Pelé, Maradona, Cafu, Roberto Carlos, Henry etc being told 'don't run with the ball'? They would have simply rebelled against such talent-limiting orders. Their coaches would have expected them to seek out attacking opportunities when the ball was at their feet from all areas of the field.

Here, both young and even older players are dissuaded from running with the ball to add to the excitement the game offers. The 'picture' of the game here is only in black and white. The addition of 'colour' might lead to mistakes! Failure should always be a concern but not a restriction on the development of young players. Unfortunately, failure often represents a knock to someone's ego in the coaching fraternity, so simplicity is sought in preference to invention.

At times, when watching our football, it seems players are being restricted by 'rubber bands' tied around their waist, allowing limited movement from their original playing positions before pulling them back again.

Good runners with the ball see and plot their path through defensive systems. Gaps are seen and pathways are plotted on the move with runs being across as well as down the field.

The ability to uncover 'hidden' pathways is not 'God given'.

It is skill that must be developed and allowed to be used by coaches in practice and transferred into games. If time on the ball in practice is discouraged, the ability to absorb 'signal' information will not be achieved and players will continue to produce colourless displays.

Coaches too often become 'talent crucifiers', often because they themselves had little playing ability and don't appreciate the benefits running with the ball can provide to a teams performance.

Positive penetrative runs with the ball can destroy well organised defensive positions in an instant. Anxiety can strike fear and indecision in the most experienced of defenders when opposing players split the gaps between them.

The talented player on the ball becomes a 'magnet' for marking players. The ability to run with the ball can draw opponents and create space for team-mates to receive or make supporting runs. Should the player on the ball penetrate the opposing defence completely then 'the world's his oyster' stardom beckons!

Percentage football has been the 'death knell' of so many talented players and for our game. Figures not fantasy have reduced so many potentially talented, young players to mundane levels of performance. Inflexible, rigid practice and playing methods have killed the little boy inside too many would be players.

Football is a game that needs impassioned coaches and players who will risk condemnation plus the bravery to provide the game with the thrills and fantasy it needs to thrive on.

We have had enough of the fumbling, futile football players present coaching methods can only offer the game. The game and public want footballer's who don't conform to mediocre standards but who inspire excite and play attractive and effective football.

Player to Watch: George Best, Northern Ireland

Some say George Best was the finest footballer in the world; others are less complimentary. However, there is no doubt he holds a position of high distinction throughout the game.

Best was an exciting unpredictable player. His nimble frame in the colours of Manchester United and Northern Ireland gave defenders all around the globe nightmares when confronting him.

His exceptional skills on the ball produced goals for himself and his colleagues. He possessed the fantastic ability of running with the ball with instant changes of direction,

stops and 'dummy' plays littering his pathways through defences. At times, he was almost impossible to stop.

Best was a non conformer both on and off the field and this unpredictability provided the uncertainty to his playing style. He knew when, how and where to express his talent during games and nothing, when these opportunities occurred, would have made him deny himself those opportunities.

Much about achieving greatness is about over-coming the fear of failure. Best had no fear of failure on the football field. His confidence was set on the firm foundations of individual skill. Best, learned those skills on the streets waste patches and playgrounds of Belfast. Copying the football idols of the period, he developed his talent to play from hours of practice, discovery and judgement. What a waste of talent it would have been had some 'trophy hunter' demanded that Best should 'play it simple' or 'don't run with the ball'. The world would not have seen his enormous talent, although, some of the defenders he mesmerised would have preferred him to have taken the easy route.

Best was a 'plotter on the move'. He saw space and penetrative opportunities whilst on the run with the ball. His game was chaos-based and unpredictable, making stopping him almost impossible.

Best did not have a repertoire of tricks. He had the ability to see space or create it by running with the ball at speed; changing direction in an instant Best, simply reapplied the skills of the street to the green turf of Old Trafford and numerous other stadia around the World.

George Best is an example of a football genius who had the strength of character when it came to football not to be taken down the road of the ordinary player. His mind and talent were destined for only one path – football immortality.

Player to Watch: Maradona, Argentina

I refer to Maradona once again. He is an example of a player who had great ability when running with the ball. Maradona could never be told to be ordinary. His game was all about playing on the limits of impossibility and he was unafraid to try the unusual no matter what the circumstances.

Success was not always possible with some of the audacious things he attempted during games but he was never afraid to try.

Ruthless marking of him was his constant companion but he rode the tackles, ran between and around opponents with consistent ease and speed, providing memorable moments for all to share.

His talents knew no boundaries, whether playing in Argentina, Spain or Italy he was capable of winning matches virtually single-handed (footed!). Once on the ball, he was able to be a child again and to reproduce, in the finest stadiums in the world, what he had done on the dusty streets of his home in Argentina as a boy. At his peak, his ability to run through opposing defences was legendary. His space and time awareness, his speed, strength and balance have all been captured on film and are a must for any young player to watch.

Unfortunately, age and poor health did what a multitude of opponents had failed to do – extinguish the golden glow of the international talent that was – Maradona.

Player to Watch: Ryan Giggs, Wales, Manchester United

How did Ryan Giggs happen? In a football culture that stifles individualism, Giggs appeared on the football scene like a long lost dinosaur.

Giggs has probably been more expressive on the football field than in his outside lifestyle. He has not 'hit the headlines' with outrageous episodes off the field but has reproduced a consistent high quality of performances for club and country on the field that have brought fame and fortune to him.

Giggs has speed and control. He uses both to great effect mostly from the left, but more so as his career has developed, from central positions.

Like all top players he is unafraid to play on the very limits of his ability. He has the quality within his game to be provider or finisher of chances. His runs with the ball bring excitement to our game that is so lacking.

More players like Ryan Giggs are needed to be produced for our domestic game. He has been a beacon of football quality on and off the field.

CHAPTER

HAVE THE SKILLS AND CONFIDENCE TO DRIBBLE PAST OPPONENTS WHEN NECESSARY AND WITH EFFECT

So often in the game today you see a player receive the ball to his feet with space around him. What does he do? He passes the ball to a colleague who is being marked. What does this player do? He passes the ball, and so it continues – pass, pass, and pass. Like factory produced 'clones' – mediocrity prevails.

Where is the individual? Where is the player who can beat an opponent and, in a single instant of individual magic, destroy the best-laid plans and strategies of the most formidable of defences?

Dribbling requires bravery.

It's not the 'beefy beast' who should command respect for lunging tackles or fierce heading but the delicate artist who, with one subtle piece of individual cleverness can outwit the meanest defender and open the tightest of defensive barriers.

Dribbling involves a special type of courage because it deals in split seconds and fractions of a centimetre and where failure is a constant companion. Accompanied by derision or abuse the dribbler who fails must reapply himself quickly to try again, for the benefits to be gained justify a limited success rate, for when successful, it can win matches!

It is important to be realistic about the skill of dribbling. The decisions of 'where and when' to dribble, are equally as important as the 'how' of doing it. Dribbling in the wrong place, at the wrong time and failing, can produce disapproval from everyone, whereas used intelligently in midfield or attacking areas of the field where failure can be retrieved, dribblers can unlock the door to major prizes.

The dribbler as already stated, needs both mental as well as physical bravery. They not only suffer condemnation from crowds, they also often receive inadequate protection from referees. Dribbling is a specialist art and needs to be carefully nurtured by the game. Like all works of art and all like all 'masterpieces', dribbling skills need to be carefully 'unwrapped', displayed and protected.

Dribbling to be really effective must produce satisfactory end products: a pass, a cross or a shot. We have all seen the 'tarnished genies' of the game who promise so much but produce so little. Frustration with them has made all sections of the game impatient and dismissive of their talent and the game has sought less gifted, but more reliable performers. Statistics, not skill, is expected to uphold the fantasy values of the game – unsurprisingly statistics don't!

In future dribbling talent must not be discredited, discarded and sacrificed for 'percentage players'. Dribblers, footballs 'knights in shining armour', must be better schooled and introduced into our game in larger numbers. The cleverness dribblers can bring to the game is, at present, missing from it and until their talent is reintroduced, our game will continue to lack quality and colour.

Running, turning, checking and screening are the basis of individualism on the ball – 'athletics with a ball'.

For too long our game has been guilty of producing the 'half player' – all skills but no athletic quality – or the athlete with limited football skills. Coaching must provide more 'total' players to the game if it is to be played with quality and style.

In football, it is not emphasised enough that 'great players' and great dribblers, need to play in the future'. What is meant by this statement is that these players are often less concerned with the immediate situation confronting them, but with the space and opportunities beyond. Like a maze, the way through must be quickly and carefully calculated and penetrated.

The movement of the ball moves defenders. A dribbler, therefore, should move the ball quickly and, at the same time, calculate the space between themselves and opponent that would allow a change of direction to be made without the defender being able to make a successful challenge for the ball. The ability to assess distance in which to perform is essential in all sports – none more so than to the dribbler in football.

Moving the ball across defenders rather than directly at them as in the past is more common today. As defenders have become more adept at their defensive roles and better physically, the dribbler has needed to unbalance opponents with clever use of speed combined with 'dummy' plays 'body swerves' and changes of direction.

Timing and space awareness are the 'hidden tools' in the dribblers workbox. It is the ability to make sound judgements in these vital areas that makes the difference between success or failure over an opponent.

Dribblers are the game's ultimate entertainers who accept the 'knife edge' challenge that sadly too few accept in the game today. We, the adoring football public, must allow them their moments of bravery, for when successful they stay in our memories forever.

Player to Watch: Sir Stanley Matthews, England

Matthew's came to be known as 'the wizard of the dribble'.

He was the ultimate football entertainer and millions of fans idolised him wherever he played. Space and time in which to receive the ball were far more

abundant during Matthews' playing career, but it is how he used that space and time that placed him in football's Hall of Fame.

Matthews, with his long baggy shorts, brought fear to all defenders against whom he played. From his usual wide, right wing position, he approached an opponent all the time noting any slight imbalance from him that Matthews would exploit with speed and penetration down the flank.

Matthews 'prepared' opponents in a sacrificial way before 'devouring' them with his touch and speed.

The Matthews' magic remains a legend in the game. His ability to unbalance opponents, burst past them and deliver crosses passes or shots has been remembered and enthused over for more than 50 years.

Matthews is an example to all young players. Here was someone who provided the game with something special that will be remembered and talked about for years to come by those fortunate enough to have seen him play.

Player to Watch: Chris Waddle, England

Waddle, combined the wizardry of the Matthews era with the more direct dribbling style of modern football.

Waddle, was basically a wide left attacking player who realised the problems he could give to defenders by playing on the right of his team but using his left foot when dribbling.

Like Matthews, his early career saw him mainly playing on the flanks. However, as his playing reputation developed and marking became more severe, he was often found more centrally. Whenever the opportunity arose for him to 'take on' an opponent he never shunned at the chance.

Using his left foot he would take the ball across defenders to affect their balance. His attention was focussed on timing and space availability for him to exploit. When he judged the opponent was unbalanced enough. Waddle would change direction in a flash leaving the defender floundering. It was a common sight to see defenders turned from side to side as Waddle changed direction and aimed 'dummy' plays at the ball.

Waddle, deserves tremendous respect for his playing skills. He had not compromised his individual ability through the 'don't days' of English football. Waddle, should be remembered as the dribbler who found success 'the wrong way round'.

Player to Watch: Ronaldo, Manchester United, Portugal

Ronaldo, reflects the changes in the modern game that the dribbler has had to address. He is skillful with tremendous athletic qualities.

Ronaldo, represents fast movement with the ball. His balance aligned to the speed of his feet round the ball produces skills that bear his particular hallmark. He has also developed an all-round game to provide meaningful end products for both himself and his teammates.

Movement wide or across the field characterises his game today. With the ball at his feet he is an awesome sight as he tantalises defenders and skips past their lunging tackles.

Bravery, not just physical but mental toughness, is obvious when watching him play. He never suffers from a loss of confidence if he fails – he is prepared to take another chance when it occurs.

For opposing teams, he has become almost impossible to counter. The 'do-it-easy' brigade should look at Ronaldo to see what can be achieved if players are coached well and given the encouragement to expand and not be restricted in their play.

Nobody has the right to deny young talent. Ronaldo is a great example of a footballer who was allowed to 'play to the music of the game'.

CHAPTER

HAVE A 'SOFT' TOUCH WHEN PASSING AND CONTROLLING THE BALL

It doesn't matter how elegant a house looks on the surface, it is only as good as the foundations on which it is built.

Important football foundations are passing and control. Unless players are daring and expert at these vital skills the whole framework of a game collapses.

Players must develop a 'love affair' with the ball. To have a 'touch like an elephant' belittles elephants and provides nothing towards the quality of the game. Great players display a superb touch, They have to because of the pressure and restricted time and space in which they are tested in competitive matches.

Control is about absorbing the pace from a pass. Being able to 'cushion' the ball and turn it in a single movement into space is an art form of its own. Being able to control the ball and change direction using any part of the body whilst under pressure and moving at speed is essential in the hectic atmosphere of top-level football. Like the delicate brushwork of an artist, the caring hands of a nurse or the tenderness of a mother for her child, the football player must produce the same sensitive touch and feel for the ball in both passing and controlling situations.

To achieve the desired results when controlling the ball, players must visualise the control required according to the ball's flight towards them. Time and space decisions are never more apparent than when controlling the ball. Body shape and awareness to produce a successful result are essential for a smooth flowing performance.

A good first touch allows for an even better second touch should it be required.

The football should not be seen as simply something made of leather and filled with air. To all great players it is far more than that, it their 'Stradivarius Violin' and playing with it must be an accomplishment, performed with care and feeling.

Passing is very much about touch and feel. Instead of the 'hammering' the ball receives when passed in our game today, it should be 'persuaded' to its target. Too often the ball is hit with little care and attention and many of our players are guilty of 'passing the buck', not the ball'.

Preparation for passing is once again so important for variation and accuracy. Poor attention to the details of body and foot positioning when passing are usually the reason for bad delivery.

Rolling, floating, bending, or chipping the ball around the field requires adjustment, balance and 'feel' for the ball. Correct passing speeds and disguised directions, can only be achieved with a 'sympathetic' touch and an imaginative mind.

Players must take more care about the quality of passing. Giving the ball away does nothing to assist in the winning of games. Simply hitting the target is not good enough; correct height and speeds combined with placement provides the receiving player with easier control and more playing options. It is annoying how easily at all levels in this country, possession of the ball is given away to the opposition.

Great passers 'feel' the ball to their team-mates from the most pressurised situations where their touch and delivery remains soft and considerate.

Throughout this book I have continuously stressed the importance of cleverness in the game. The time for over-simplistic, straight-lined methods must end. Disguise, variation and improved passing standards must be taught if our game is to develop a 'framework' of passing quality to provide success in the future.

The use of the outside of either foot when passing the ball should be common-place throughout our game, but it isn't! In fact this type of pass is probably one of the least seen skills in the British game. The use of the instep is far more common, mainly because coaches give it priority. Why I don't understand.

Passing with the outside of the feet is easier to shape up to; quicker to use; and allows for a better running action to follow once the pass has been made.

Passes should be played as much as possible on the ground, however, this is not always possible or necessary. But generally, good passers – individuals and teams, play the ball around on the ground.

Two of my coaching colleagues sum up passing well: The first says: 'If God had meant the ball to be played in the air so much, the sky would been green not blue!' The other says: 'I tell my players I want them to pass the ball under the grass, but, if they find that too difficult I tell them to pass the ball as near to under the grass as possible!'

Player to Watch: Franz Beckenbauer, Germany

Known as the 'Kaizer', Beckenbauer played the role of 'sweeper' with the skillful quality of a more attacking player. His ability on the ball combined with an

astute football mind allowed him to bring more variety into his performances than could be seen from almost anyone else.

Beckenbauer's career brought him numerous trophies for club and country. He typified the elegance of the game and he projected an unflappable image in the most heated situations.

Immediate control and a wide range of passing skills or runs with the ball were a consistent part of his game.

So many great players could be mentioned in any of the chapters of this book. Beckenbauer is one of these greats of the game.

His instant control of the ball and variety of passes played with 'arrogant', effortless style made him a superb player. Beckenbauer was a precise passer of the ball; speeds, heights, placements, disguise, accuracy, and imagination were all there in his game. The use of all parts of his feet made him able to deliver the ball quickly whenever necessary.

Beckenbauer portrayed an aristocratic radiance in the manner and style in which he played the game. All young players should watch videos of this wonderful player in action. At the highest level of competitive play, he produced performances for clubs and country that portrayed a cool and collected approach to the game.

His individual skills and superb game understanding incorporating his intelligent 'reading' of the game, lifted him above the 'rough and tumble' so often offered as quality football.

Player to Watch: Bobby Moore, England

I was fortunate enough to be at West ham United with Bobby Moore during the late 1950s and early 1960s. We were both in the youth and reserve teams before progressing into first team football. Geoff Hurst and Martin Peters, his team-mates in our successful world cup team of 1966 were also young players at the club at that time.

West Ham's 'Academy of Football' status derived from the young players who came through the development programme at that time and has continued successfully over many years since.

Bobby was not one of those players who could have played in a variety of positions. His qualities were his command of defensive play and his ability to switch defence into attack with a quick control and effective passes delivered over varying lengths.

It was obvious from the earliest days of his development that lack of pace could be a limiting factor in his progress. Because of this, he practiced to 'speed-up' his game by improving his understanding and awareness. He became astute at intercepting passes and winning the ball.

He mastered the ball, controlling it quickly and used it effectively and quickly. Probably, it was the range and accuracy of his delivery skills that was obvious to all who watched him play. He could pick out the vital pass and deliver it with either foot over any distance with superb quality.

At West Ham, he developed an almost telepathic partnership with Hurst. The ultimate of this 'chemistry' between the two players was Moore's long pass to Hurst from a quickly-taken free kick in the 1966 World Cup Final from which Hurst scored his first goal and England's equaliser against Germany.

From his position in the heart of West Ham's defence, Moore was the ultimate 'leader' of play. He continually seemed to step in and take the ball off the toes of attacking players and follow this with a telling pass.

It was a joy playing with Moore. He always gave you the ball early. In doing so he made the game easier for his team-mates. He controlled and passed the ball – the foundation of the game – with masterly ease and perfection.

CHAPTER

COMBINE CLEVERLY AND IMAGINATIVELY WITH COLLEAGUES

Individual skill is the 'diamond' of quality performance. Imaginative, combined team play is the 'precious substance' in which it is set.

Whether team movement involves several players linking play together or a singular action on or off the ball by a player, it is movement that establishes good ball possession; creates openings and causes problems for defending players.

Achieving the balance between over-complication and obvious, predictable play is vital in order to achieve consistent success in the game. Whether combining in passing sequences or supporting individual play, it is movement that provides positive linkage for team possession.

Combining together can be a simple movement to create an angle to receive, or a longer run to exploit an attacking opportunity. In all examples, it is supportive, combined movement that embellishes individual skill in the game.

Combined play requires minds to work in unison. 'A good football brain' is an apt description for being able to recognise, analyse and act on situations within the game. As the game increases in pace and complexity the ability to absorb, digest and dissect information becomes more difficult, but even more important.

In every-day business, increased levels of production are achieved by creating uniformity in production methods – robots and computers are used extensively. In football, speed is added to our game with the use of 'direct playing' methods making it fast and 'system-conscious'.

Our game has become far more predictable and less attractive to watch. Players have become fraught with fear, often resembling the 'robot-controlled' production lines of business, not sporting worlds. 'Straight-lined' thinking, requiring straight-lined play, has brought monotony not fantasy to our game. The same can be said for other countries who have followed in our footsteps.

Some coaches have stated that 'direct play' methods pander to our national characteristics; I find that difficult to believe. We have always shown a broad and open approach to life; why should our football be constrained when the game allows for a 360 degree playing opportunity.

As adults we teach our children to assess situations and formulate good decisions. We certainly would not condone our children being told to 'walk across a busy road without looking'! Why then, should our young and senior players be ushered into a game style that displays similar robotic responses?

By forcing a fast, repetitive game / style onto our players, coaches have 'killed' both 'individualism' and clever, combined qualities in our game. A combative game/style resembling the 'trench warfare' of World War 1 best illustrates our current playing of the game. This 'red bloodied' approach must be an ingredient in our play, not the sole answer we have to the questions the game asks. More compassionate and better-informed Generals introduced artful movement into modern warfare to probe weaknesses in opposing, defences through which, with speed and dexterity, their forces could penetrate to provide the certainty of victory.

It seems football educators abroad place more emphasis on developing playing styles that balance conveniently between the futile boredom of chess-like' passing and the rugged predictability of 'direct play'. They have concluded that possession in the attacking third is unlikely to be maintained from single passes delivered from too far back. Shorter and more precise movement of the ball through the field from back to front, creates better linkage and support with better chances of attempts on goal.

Coaches and players should know their sport and the importance of combined team play. Our fans must also learn the importance of combined team play through the field. Instead of demanding a game style of the past based upon effort, supporters must be encouraged to show more patience with the players and allow a more flowing style which involves a suitable mixture of long and shorter playing methods. Winning is important to players and their fans but winning regularly and with style is even more important.

It was Jimmy Greaves who first said, 'football's a funny old game'. But too often it's those who are involved in it or watch it who are the 'funny ones'. So many who say they love the game commit it to mundane levels of mediocrity by demanding a game/style lacking in class and quality.

If we continue to demand, simplistic, predictability and play 'percentage football', we will 'kill the music' of the game forever. High levels of individual skill increases tactical playing options. Our game must provide the first for the second to thrive. In Italy, their passionate fans expect their teams to play with both individual fantasy and team collectiveness. In France, their crowds expect a cultured football style of slick movement interwoven with individual cleverness. Throughout most parts of the 'footballing globe' quality of performance has been expected to accompany the positive result.

Unfortunately, our fans show a worrying lack of patience and desire in seeing our game establish a better playing quality than at present. Let's be braver; let's be more stylish both on and off the field. Let's be more tolerant towards the true needs and qualities of this fantastic game. Like the diamond set in gold, let individualism and combined play be the ingredients of a sport rich with creative and exciting possibilities.

Player to Watch: Rivelino, Brazil

Once again, I make no apologises for naming a Brazilian player in the category of an individual capable of orchestrating team play. Rivelino fits the picture admirably.

With his influential 'baton', (his left foot) he was the constructive influence in providing the attacking framework of Brazilian football during his illustrious playing career. He was excellent in consolidating ball possession and then quickly exploiting any opportunity with intelligent passing and movement. Simple possession play was made to look attractive given the Rivelino brand of style and authority. Small movements to provide angles to support others or space for himself were central to his playing style. From his midfield role he displayed both patience and poise that linked parts of his team together in preparation for speedier penetrative opportunities.

Whether supporting others or involving himself in attacking or defensive play, he was constantly on the move for 90 minutes. Alongside so many other Brazilian and world stars he stands high in the estimation of those who admire true quality.

Rivelino was a footballing 'architect'.

He could build a football edifice from seemingly barren surroundings. His football structure provided both Brazil and the world with tremendous entertainment and winning results.

From a languid almost lazy stroll and easy 'loan' of the ball, to swift penetration and 'hostile' finishing, Rivelino typified the very best of Brazilian 'total' football magic.

Player to Watch: Gianfranco Zola, Italy

Zola had to be outstanding in so many of the skills required for top-class professional football. His skills were protected by a strong physique and a mental toughness that shielded his game against fierce tackling defenders.

Like, David against Goliath, Zola would slay his bigger defensive foes with creative, imaginative football genius both on and off the ball. In games he was usually in the thickest of the action, using his skill and awareness to unlock the tangle of bodies that so often surrounded him.

Zola transformed his natural, street-learned game onto the football stadia of the world. Like so many of his generation the chaos of the street brought opportunity on the football field. As in the congested street games that he played during his junior years, Zola, found the 'pathways' through equally congested defences. His ability to 'see and plot' his way through a mêlée of fierce tackles and defensive cover was a memorable sight.

The street games developed Zola's 'radar'. The 'signals' he received allowed him to quickly interpret and act on them effectively. His individual qualities were often the key to clever linkage with supporting players. He was a master of the art of drawing opponents to him before threading passes to colleagues to score.

Zola used skill to open the door of the most efficient of defences. His brilliance was his ability to recognise the time to release the ball.

Zola, whose streets were really paved with gold!

Player to Watch: Johann Cruyff, Holland

Cruyff, was a product of Ajax development history. He is a great example of an intelligent person using that intelligence both off the field in his private life and in the biggest stadia in the most prestigious tournaments. Cruyff stressed his opinions strongly and fought his 'football battles' with astute cleverness and skillful poise. He was gifted with a superb physique; this allied to an array of exciting skills made him an exciting player to watch throughout his playing career.

There have been many players who have had similar playing qualities as Cruyff, but most lacked his football intellect. He was an obvious captain for club and country and was able to influence games through his ability to link comfortably in team play or produce individual skill as the game required.

As I have already emphasised throughout the book, great players see opportunities and act on them in a decisive and positive fashion; in fact they make the difficult look easy!

Cruyff, combined easily within team patterns-of-play and he was a centrepiece for most attacking and defensive situations at club and international levels. His introduction of the 'Cruyff-turn' to the game as well as his cunning inter-linkage with team-mates earned him football's highest accolades.

Dutch football is admired in all parts of the world. It requires high individual skill and intelligent combined team play. Although only a small country with a small population, Holland is a giant of the game.

Cruyff, represents the very best of Dutch football; a huge talent from a small but highly respected football nation.

Player to Watch: Deco, Barcelona, Portugal

Deco, represents the modern game's better qualities. He plays with a physical zest that contains all the elements of a great player.

Deco, earns his football opportunities through hard physical performances allowing him to select from a 'menu' of playing options. From a successful tackle to an artful pass or delicate dribble, Deco, has the immediacy of greatness in his game.

He displays wonderful qualities in the tightest situations with his skill on and off the ball. He is capable of involving himself in clever goal assists or to be at the 'sharp end' of goal scoring.

Although relatively small, he produces big performances for club and country. Deco, has the game of football nicely organised. He earns time and space for himself with his highly competitive playing manner, which in turn provides him the chance to use his subtle playing talent in individual situations, or with creative linkage with his teammates.

Deco, a clever player, cloaked with a fierce, competitive attitude.

CHAPTER

KEEP POSSESSION OF THE BALL IN ALL AREAS OF THE FIELD - WHEN NO ATTACKING ADVANTAGE IS POSSIBLE

We fight to qualify for the finals of major cup competitions (European/World). The qualifying matches for these competitions are played over a two-year period during our autumn, winter and spring months. The climatic conditions during this time of the year are conducive to our 'up and at 'em' game style; with games spread conveniently throughout the whole qualifying period.

When it comes to the finals, however, these are played in the peak summer months, in countries where fans can enjoy both the football and the warm summer sunshine with games following quickly on each other.

During these finals, we always hear the same criticism of our teams. 'We keep giving the ball away!' Our inability to retain ball possession doesn't just occur overnight prior to these competition finals, it is an ingrained fault within our playing methodology. Poor quality ball retention cannot be cured by trying to play differently over the short period of the final stretch of a competition, when the whole preceding period has been devoted to fast, give-away football in our domestic leagues!

Football is not an exact science. If it were the game would only consist of kick-offs and goals; no mistakes being made. Despite numerous factors that contrive to limit performance, the game must be played attractively and effectively to entertain and win.

Ball possession is a vital ingredient in the playing quality of players and teams. Losing or giving the ball away easily, is something only poor players and poor teams do!

The goal has a 'magnetic' attraction. The shortest and quickest direct route satisfies too many too often in our country. Playing the ball forward at every occasion irrespective of better ball retention possibilities is the 'lazy-mans' method of playing.

Let me quickly point out; it isn't wrong to play fast direct football, but it is wrong to be non-selective in the game and play fast, direct football all the time!

Bill Shankly, summed it up when describing Liverpool's experience playing in Europe 'Your players must realise you can't score every time you're in possession of the ball, and – when you give the ball away against good teams, they don't' give it back to you easily!'

The over-emphasis throughout the development years on winning has delivered passion not possession to our game. This only shows an ignorance about the game. Speed and physical effort, un-constrained within a second-rate tactical framework reflects the general quality of both individual and team performance expected here. In Britain, the founders of the game, the crowds do not relish a game- style based on sophisticated tactics as do their foreign counterparts. Fans here demand easy, fast, forward movement of the ball into the opposing team's penalty box – and for their team to win irrespective of the quality of the performance.

Until crowds allow players to play in a more controlled and skillful manner our game here will never flourish at domestic or national levels. All speed and no brains, equals fast failure! Being able to govern the ball in order to prepare more patiently for better attacking opportunities is essential for sustained success. The long, forward pass, when correctly used, does two important things. One; it relieves pressure near your own goal and transfers pressure onto your opponents goal; two; it creates space inside your own half of the field to drop back into and develop play from.

Quick closing down on back players (pressurisation) has evolved in Britain far more so than in most other parts of the world. In order to intimidate defenders and their inferior skill levels, pressure applied in the defending third means possible loss of the ball near one's own goal with obvious disastrous results. To overcome pressure play, defenders played the ball as quickly and as directly back into their opponents defending area and with the rest of their team; pushed up quickly to return the pressure on their opponents.

This to and fro football has never really been eliminated from our game. The long ball is still the preferred pass from our back players even when time and space allow for other options to be used.

We will never achieve true world-class standards until back players become better footballer's and increase their attacking options from back areas. Back players have more time on the ball and more space than anyone else on the field to develop better playing options. Poor individual skill combined with a lack of game knowledge, deprives them and their teammates of the use of increased choices for the game. The lack of confidence and quality on the ball of back players directly affects the playing standard of those players in more advanced positions. Poor service from the back limits playing quality, style, and team results.

The main runway at any airport would not be a pretty sight if all incoming aircraft were allowed to descend onto it in a disorderly scramble. In order that take-offs and landings take place without a chaotic mêlée, aircraft are asked to wait in pre-determined 'stacking areas' some distance from the airport. They are advised to circle at varying heights before being called in to fill a space in the flight path for their final approach for landing.

I hope this analogy with aviation is appropriate because like aviations 'stacking areas' football's 'play-round areas' fulfil a similar role. If correctly and quickly used, the ball can be transferred from areas of congestion and pressure around to players in space on the other side of the field so that possession is maintained and forward penetrative options might be better achieved.

Uncoordinated attempts to penetrate forward cannot always be made immediately a team gets possession of the ball. Unfortunately, too many of the games seen here are an example of the mess a runway would look like if all the incoming flights tried to land without following an organised approach and landing procedure.

Impatient to 'land' the ball forward has been and still is, a debilitating factor in our playing of the game at all levels. Coaching, has given little thought or time to the importance of ball possession and the significance of the 'stacking areas' or 'play-round areas' of football. If the ball is to be retained and better forward service and penetration is to occur more time must be spent schooling our wayward footballing 'aviators.'

There are four play-round areas on the football field:

1.   The deepest level
The ball being passed around the back close to goal using the goalkeeper to redirect the ball coming to him from one side of the field to the other side.

2.   The back level
The ball being passed around the back by the back players inside their own half of the field.

3.   The mid-level
The ball being played around the field inside the opponents half.

4.   The forward level
The ball being played around inside the attacking third, close to the opposing penalty area.

From each of the 'play-round areas' described all players in possession of the ball must search for the opportunity to break forward quickly through spaces in the opposing teams formation. But if the opportunity is not there, or an attempt to penetrate is thwarted, then patience and ball possession must continue around the 'play-round' areas until another forward penetration becomes available.

The possibility to 'overload' by back players into mid-field has become almost a lost art in the game. The importance and significance of this tactic is little understood or used but is a useful tool in a team's playing style should it be attempted.

Penetration from back positions into mid-field allows better possession of the ball to be achieved throughout the team. It also provides more options to both the man on the ball as well as to those off it. The length of passing reduces as the back player moves forward to mid-field. The distance between himself and his forward colleagues become less. An option to the longer pass is available!

We have so much more to do in order that our future players have a better playing pedigree. From a game of straight-lined playing to one enriched by 360 degree opportunities, coaching must bring lustre and brilliance back into football's shop windows.

Our game need's players who are comfortable in possession of the ball and teams that play possession football in a positive manner. In so doing, goalscoring chances throughout games would increase considerably.

Football must cast off the yoke of academic mishandling. Fifty years of unproductive, unrealistic, practice producing laboured, 'give-the-ball-away-football is enough. It's time for change – drastic change!!

Player to Watch: Alan Hansen, Scotland

I can remember a young player asking Alan Hansen the question 'Why do you always look so confident in possession of the ball?'

Alan's simple reply was 'Because I can use both feet and opponents can't put me under pressure'.

Hansen was a rare breed of player not usually seen in the British game. A footballing central defender, he was probably the most important player in the Liverpool team of the 1980's.

His ability to play constructively at all times allowed both his club and country to develop attacking play from deep defensive situations in which other less talented players would normally have given the ball away.

Hansen, was a good 'stopper' of opponents attacking play, but a great 'starter' of his own team's offensive play. Retaining possession and probing for chances to penetrate forward with the ball at his feet or with a deft pass, was the essence of his game. Giving the ball away cheaply was not something he was prepared to do.

His support positions for surrounding teammates was far superior than offered by players in a similar role. Whether dropping off deep to create or use space, or searching for 'linkage' opportunities in midfield and further forward, he was the exception to the rule when compared with his contemporaries.

It is my opinion great teams start by being accomplished at the back- both defensively and offensively! Hansen provided a playing standard for his teams that few others have matched. From his performance, he made the game easier to play for others in his team.

He was a shining example to all young players playing at the back and who are encouraged to 'hit it long and often' to play with more cultured elegance.

His self-belief and independent character made him lift his personal performances well above the mediocre standards so often expected of central defenders.

Alan Hansen, the complete player. A clear example of how it should be done.

Player to Watch: Xavi, Barcelona, Spain

In the modern game of cut-and-thrust football, time and space awareness is a price-less gift. Xavi has that gift. In the more cultured tempo of international football, or in the fiercely competitive domestic and European club football scene, Xavi has that playing quality that lifts his performance above the usual.

He has a wonderful 'eye' for space and then being able to execute subtle runs and passes with the ball. He is an 'anchor' player for club and country and provides each with a solidity of possession – play from his mid-field position.

Xavi rarely gives the ball away. There is a continual stream of positive play emanating from him, and his teammates benefit enormously from both his playing guile, as well as his competitive spirit.

Both on the ball and in supporting play, he provides an inspiring example of a top-class modern player, who although under the same pressures as everyone else, still provides his teams and the game with a cameo of skill and movement that has positive ball-possession as a central core.

Player to Watch: Kenny Dalglish, Scotland

I have used Kenny Dalglish as an example who, in the most congested and hard-fought area of the field – the attacking third, was a genius at ball possession.

At this 'sharp end' of the game, getting the ball to 'stick' whilst under sever pressure from defenders, is not easy. Clubs spend huge amounts of time and money to locate and buy players with this ability. If the player can also score goals – he's worth a fortune!

Dalgish was capable of performing both sides of the attacking game! He could hold the ball and provide assists for his teammates, or score goals himself.

Too often passes into front players are lost through poor control, lack of physical strength, or poor awareness. With possession breaking down so easily and so often team movement fails to function properly.

To have a player of Dalglish's class in such an important area of the field gave Liverpool and Scotland an important 'edge' to their game. Giving the ball away in and around the penalty area was not something Dalglish was prepared to do and he used every part of his skill and physical strength to hold the ball himself or link up with others.

Scotsmen are supposed to be careful when it comes to money issues. Dalglish, must have seen the game of football through the eyes of a Scottish banker for he 'saved' the ball for himself; 'loaned' it to others but 'received' high interest payments through the goals he scored or assisted.

They say 'greatness is about making the difficult look easy' well, if that's the case, Dalglish, stands supreme.

Liverpool FC had many outstanding players throughout the Dalglish 'reign'. On their day their football quality was exceptional. In a leading role, at the heart of so much of their success was Kenny Dalglish, a 'miserly' master of possession.

CHAPTER

BE AWARE OF 'OVERLOAD' SITUATIONS WHENEVER POSSIBLE - WITH AND WITHOUT THE BALL

Whilst driving my car I listened to a radio commentary of an international Rugby match played at Twickenham between England and France. It was interesting to compare the difference between the commentary details of this game to the commentary on Association Football.

The Rugby commentary broadcast was much more specialised, with more emphasis provided on team tactics and the methods employed to gain tactical advantage over the opposition by both sides. Why? The 'overloading' of play to add an extra player or players into a situation should be automatic in all teams games; but in football it isn't taught, used or discussed enough!

'Overloading' as a tactical tool is a rarely seen occurrence on the British football scene. We see and hear little about it from coaches, players, 'pundits' and fans. Its lack of use would give the impression that 'overloading' has a limited effect on the game. On the contrary, 'overloading', purposefully carried out can be highly significant in both individual and team performance.

As already mentioned in an earlier chapter, the ability to break forward from deeper playing positions to support or carry the ball should be encouraged by coaches and fans alike.

Bravery and understanding must be shown by all involved in the game to exploit 'overload' opportunities in the game. 'Long Ball Mania', reduced the need and consigned chances to play with cleverness to the dustbin. The lid must be removed and 'overloading' be allowed to display its importance in successful football.

To expect intelligent movement with or without the ball; to create extra players into attacking situations should be second nature to all involved in the game. Because our coaching 'hierarchy' preferred a more direct approach to playing methods, the use and benefits of 'overloading' have remained ignored. To compound the problem, low skill quality, only able to satisfy our mundane playing style, is not prepared to risk itself beyond limited boundaries of responsibility. Therefore movement remains solid and inflexible throughout most of our teams.

'Keep a shape', is constantly shouted to players during matches. Mostly, this 'shape' is kept by denying players the chance to – change places! Lack of bravery, skills and understanding produces a solid, lineal predictability. Tidiness and 'packaged mediocrity' is preferred over movement involving clever interchange and positional rotation.

Watching a junior match between two teams of boys at Under 12 level, I was told that these boys had been coached from 8 years of age at this club's professional, junior section. Everything concerning the organisation and control of the game was correctly applied. It was a beautiful day, the field was the right size, so were the goals, the surface was flat, the lush green grass was perfectly mowed and both teams looked the part as they warmed-up in their smart playing kit.

The referee started the game.

Both teams played 'nice' football. When a player received the ball – he passed it to a teammate, who also passed it, and so it continued until the ball was lost. It was frightening to watch! Here were two teams of 'uncut diamonds' not being allowed to 'sparkle' independently; they were forced to play like 'faulty gems' only for industrial use, rather than for valuable jewellery.

Such a sight is all too common in both junior and subsequently therefore, senior football in this country. At a time when young players should be encouraged to maximise their talent they are impressed into a rigid playing conformity. It isn't surprising skill is in such short supply that our senior game relies on foreign imports to provide it!

Football's coaching 'hierarchy' over the years have found it impossible to set a recognisable path forward. From the days of rote-learned, unrealistic drill practices, to the nightmare of 'direct play' with all its implications; we now move into the 'pass-pass-pass period'.

In its present, mistaken form, development of our youngsters will still not produce skillful individuals. Who wants to remember a good under 12 team? It's aspiring, individual greatness we remember!

Before my eyes that day was the calculated production of footballs next group of 'clones'; 'packaged players', moving in order along a robotic assembly line – 'commercial vans not expensive sports cars'!

What is constantly left unappreciated within coaching are the words; 'space and time'; magical words, all involved in the game should explore and revere. Those young players mentioned earlier had no appreciation or understanding of space and time and how to use it in the game; because they had never been taught! How, when, where to develop attacking play by using time and space available is essential in the learning process for all players. The use of 'overloading' makes the game simpler to play and improves the playing standards throughout the team.

Correctly and speedily applied, the linking of an additional player or players into attacking moves forces defenders into an almost 'no win' situation. By 'overloading' to produce 2 v 1, 3 v 2, 4 v 3 etc situations around the ball, the attacking team gives itself more alternatives, thus allowing more positive and effective attacking play.

In order to retain defensive 'safety' when 'overloading' is being used, the player or players not directly involved must be prepared to change positions with those players who have moved from their normal position on the field. By rotating positions in this way 'holes' are not left in the defence should possession be lost.

Football is like a lottery; if you don't buy a ticket you cant win a prize! Similarly, if you don't see and take the chance to 'overload' when possible during the game of football, you are unlikely to pick up winning results at the end!

Football is also about problems; setting them for the opposition, and solving problems set by the opposition. The use of 'overloading' by an attacking team, sets an almost impossible problem for opposing teams to solve!

How gratifying it would be to know that your team has the playing formula to (a) create almost impossible situations for the opposition to solve; (b) make the game easier for your players; (c) give yourself a bigger chance to win.

'Overloading' is an absolute necessity in the playing quality of top players and top teams. At all levels of the game, let's read more about it; hear more about it; teach it more; see it happen more.

Player to Watch: Lucio, Brazil

Once again, I have given a Brazilian player as an example of quality football talent. Lucio has emerged for both club and country as a truly outstanding player.

Although he plays as a central defender, he is unlike most others who play in this position. Lucio is a complete footballer; he has to defend well – he's a defender primarily; but he is also a fine, individually skillful player, who has no problem or lack of confidence when on the ball.

Lucio is a fine example of how a back player can break forward, with or without the ball to 'overload' areas in front of him. His ability on the ball allows him to utilise the space and time available and he takes every opportunity to 'burst' through gaps in front of him to supply passes to his team mates, or take chances at goal for himself.

Lucio plays the 'whole' game.

He is not content to sit at the back to head or kick the ball away. He can do that with ease when required to do so but the added dimensions of his game provide an exciting and inspiring difference to the game when seeing him play.

Lucio is a brave player who is not satisfied in just being like other defenders. He has the skills so he uses them – to great effect!

Player to Watch: Steven Gerrard, Liverpool, England

There are too few English players I place in the category – Players to Watch. I do not think Gerrard is yet at the point in his career where it could be said he is a great player. He does however, set a fine example of the ability to 'overload' from midfield positions into the difficult and congested attacking areas of the field.

For his club, Liverpool, he finds no problem linking with his forwards explosively to 'overload' in the final third to score or set up assists for others. He has the patience of the hunter who watches and waits for the chance to spring forward for the kill. He sees these chances and acts decisively, both on the ball or to link up with another player.

For England, he finds difficulty in making the link with the front players. This is not necessarily his fault as our front players do not keep the ball well enough and linkage with them is poor. However, when the occasion does occur, Gerrard, will be looking to penetrate forward past floundering defenders to 'overload' advanced attacking situations.

England must improve their playing quality and adjust their playing methodology to allow a player like Gerrard to reach the highest playing levels his ability deserves.

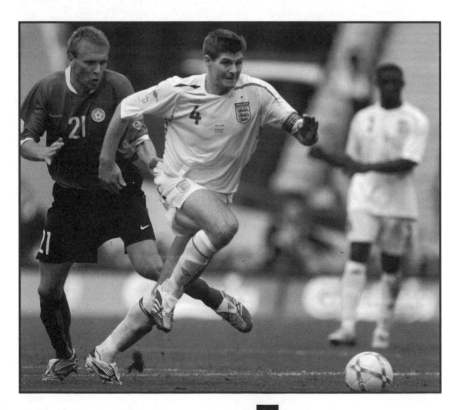

Player to Watch: Roberto Carlos, Brazil

As an example of the modern 'attacking defender' Roberto Carlos has few equals. His playing quality: both physical and skillful underline his tremendous talent. Like many of the players i have selected as examples of particular aspects of the game, Carlos could virtually play in any position and produce a top class performance.

Some argue about limitations in his defensive qualities that he sometimes gets caught out of position through his desire to 'overload' attacking opportunities. Carlos, is a Brazilian; staying back and not expressing himself through his exciting ability is certainly not for him, nor the ardent Brazilian football public.

Space; be it wide or central is never left 'unexplored territory' by him, with or without the ball. At every opportunity he involves himself in seeking attacking advantages (overloading) against out-numbered opponents.

Roberto Carlos is all about exciting, clever football. He satisfies the example of Brazilian colour in the game through his skill and speed. He also provides intelligent tactical understanding that, at times, makes him almost impossible to contain.

He is a fearful adversary, capable of exploiting the smallest fissure in the most solid of defences. 'Overloading is a cornerstone of his game – Long may it be so!!

CHAPTER

FINISH POSITIVELY AND ACCURATELY FROM ALL HEIGHTS AND DISTANCES

No better use of the lottery analogy can be found than in the context of finishing in football; for if you don't take the chance that offers itself, you don't score. However there is a clear distinction between the gamble of where a winning ticket might be issued and the more predictable and recognisable positioning from which goals are scored.

There are thousands of football coaching manuals detailing the techniques involved in kicking and heading and how these can be suitably adapted to goal scoring. All these books describe the 'how' to do something which is, of course, vitally important if a successful skillful outcome is to be achieved, but behind every undertaking there must be a real desire on behalf of the performer to make it happen.

Goal scoring, above anything else, is about 'wanting to score'. It is the very catalyst of the game, for scoring is the ultimate object of the game, and therefore, tends to be the most difficult part of it to master.

Goal scorers are not all physically alike; the physical shape is not necessarily important. A smaller player tends to need more speed to overcome a height disadvantage. The taller player can add the alternative of heading as an option in attacking play. In all cases however scoring is about getting; into goal scoring positions; being prepared to score; and having the skills to score.

'A faint heart never won a football match'

The bravery of the prolific goal scorer is unquestionable. To score goals regularly he must go into areas where knocks and physical contact will most certainly occur. He must take any chance that offers itself but be unaffected by missing a chance and not allow failure to unsettle or deter him. The top goal scorer's courage is reflected by his natural instinct to try again to do the most difficult in the game – score!

Goal scoring then, has a great deal to do with attitude of mind. Some players get their thrills in being recognised as a provider of chances for others to convert. The mean goal scorer, has his concentration bent on 'hitting the net' and will focus mentally towards that outcome. The great player has the combined quality to create assists or score as the situation demands.

Positioning is the secret of goal scoring success. Before goal scorers can celebrate a goal they must first find the position from which to score from. In practice sessions they must learn to anticipate the likely space the ball can go into and make sure they are in there. Unless the ability to 'read' these situations is acquired, goal scoring becomes irregular not prolific.

Once in a goal scoring position, goal scorers must quickly assess; flight, speed, angle of the ball and the space and time in which they have to work. Goals scored before millions of viewers may look simple, but are the product of hours of practice. Practice-makes-permanent sums up the goal scoring art for it is only through continuous, realistic goal scoring practice that the goal scorer can achieve and maintain the scoring 'edge'.

It's no good having a desire to score, finding the correct position to score, but then not being prepared to score. All top goal scorers are prepared to take the chance from any distance. goal scorers are not surprised when the chance comes along; they are ready for it! This early preparation allows them to decide quickly the skill required to despatch the ball goalwards.

All of the aspects concerning the actual act of goal scoring can be summed up in one word – 'signals'. From the beginning, goal scorers absorb information of various types relating to the game in general and, for them; the information or 'signals' involved in goal scoring. These 'signals' were 'received and deciphered' almost unconsciously during the competitive street, practice play games of the past by the goal scoring, immortals of those days. Coaching has not reproduced the same realism into finishing practice (due to possible injury risks) and so, goal scoring 'signals' have not been realistically acquired. It is time more thought was given to coaching finishing with more realism involved!

The book features the element of bravery within the game; not just the physical but the mental bravery players must possess to reach the top. This psychological toughness is displayed most when it comes to goal scoring. Fear of failure does not sit heavily on the shoulders of prolific goal scorers. Criticism must not be allowed to deter them from seeking out the next chance.

Throughout goal scorers' careers there will almost certainly be barren periods but good coaching, self-belief and good service from teammates will eventually improve these depressing periods. But in the end it is the individual who overcomes the problems. goal scorers act on information received and interpret those 'signals' by adjusting the kicking, heading skill that best suits the circumstance to put the ball into the net. Like a set of golf clubs, goal scorers must produce the appropriate angle and power to the ball according to the situation confronting them.

In today's game, most goal scorers are just 'patient predators', rather than 'football thoroughbreds'. Patience, not overall performance is their contribution as they wait positioned on the edge of opposing defences, for the chance to spring into the space behind defenders, to often, this being their main contribution to team play. This lack of involvement is tolerated as long as goals are scored; when goals are not forthcoming from them, team results and general performance suffers.

I believe goal scorers should be as complete in their playing ability as is possible. The area in which they compete is the most demanding and requires the highest playing qualities, not just runners and fighters. Team linkage would improve with goal scoring being shared around the team more.

The scoring of goals must not be made the responsibility of the few. The desire and opportunity to 'find the net' should be open to all within teams. Our game style must become more flexible with all our players more comfortable on the ball prepared to take the chance should it fall to them

But no matter who scores, the elation makes up for all the hard work, criticism and disappointments. Our game needs far more of the type of player who can be providers as well as finishers. All players should be able to enjoy that special feeling of scoring a goal, or two or three!

Player to Watch: Pelé, Brazil

I could have placed Pelé in any one of the categories in this book (even goalkeeper) as an example of the topic. He was indeed, a special player, with a special character and charisma.

I decided on using Pelé, as an example of goal scoring because he not only scored an incredible number of goals himself, his wonderful playing ability allowed him to be a supplier of goals for others around him too.

Much, quite rightly, has been written about Pelé. His extra-ordinary ability made him the greatest footballer ever in most peoples' estimation. Something, I feel, has never really been mentioned enough about him was his total lack of selfishness. His marvellous ability was to make it easy for him to select the correct option, to finish or provide, with casual ease. He didn't need to 'goal-hang' and await chances provided by others to score. He joined in team play, combining cleverly with others to support team movement – Brazilian Style!

Pelé's ability could 'make a minute out of a second or a meter out of a centimetre'. His awareness of space, combined with a superb touch and wonderful physique, allowed him to 'manufacture' goal pathways and finishing shapes quickly and more easily than other mere mortals.

Pelé scored goals at the very top and toughest level of the professional game. Throughout his illustrious career his individual skill created goals of every conceivable type for himself. Although Pelé must have had a fierce inner determination to succeed which was reflected in his scoring history, he played the game; 'the beautiful game' as he described it, with bravery! His skill will be remembered for the colour it provided to the game, his scoring is legendary; but it is his total football quality and his lack of selfishness that stands out.

Pelé was a total footballer, he could score goals irrespective of circumstances. His counterparts scored goals because of circumstances. Both are great but he was the greatest.

Player to Watch: Jimmy Greaves, England

I was fortunate to play several games with Greaves in England's Under 18 team. I was also unfortunate to play against him when our club sides met in domestic competitions.

Greaves became a big name in the game from an early age with his club – Chelsea. Brought up in London's eastern suburbs, he played and learned the game in the streets. He developed, like so many others youngsters of the day, the ability to control and run with the ball at his feet in congested playing areas. The ability remained with him throughout his career as he progressed from club to country.

Playing for England Youth (U18) I can remember giving him the ball near the half-way line and watch him zigzag past numerous defenders before rolling the ball past a stranded goalkeeper. The ability to score goals of this calibre became a hallmark of his time in the game.

Greaves had both skill and speed. Combined with these he had perfected from his junior days, the 'cunning eye' to recognise the ways through congested spaces. Where most would pass the ball, Greaves would wriggle his way between defenders, the ball seemingly tied to his feet. Although not tall, he also scored goals with his head. In crowded penalty areas he was a 'sniffer' of space and opportunity; whilst others stood and watched, he moved in and scored! In his career he scored many memorable goals. He was an artist of 'passing' the ball into the goal. So many of his goals were made to look easy but it was his background of street football that made the difficult look easy.

Greaves tended to be a 'goal hanger'. He was not seen playing deep or dropping off to receive the ball. He played close to the defenders and challenged them with his skill and speed in dangerous areas near their goal.

Greaves was different from Pelé. Although he had the all-round ability to involve himself more in team play he preferred the frontline attacking role. He was a huge talent who is still idolised by fans at all the clubs for whom he played.

Player to Watch: Gerd Müller, Germany

Müller was not a sophisticated player. Nobody could honestly say he played the game elegantly and with poise. However, he was a lethal goal scorer!

It takes all sorts to be a goal scorer and I use Müller as an example of goal scoring not because of his skillful qualities, but for his mental determination that focussed him so intently on scoring that it overcame his lack of skill.

Müller scored goals off all parts of his anatomy. Skillfully, he was not the most creative of players but he developed a single mindedness and with it, an awareness to be where the ball was going. He attacked the space around the opposing goalkeeper; his idea obviously being 'the Goalkeeper should be near the ball, so I'll be there too'. Goalkeepers naturally need to be near the ball to catch or save it. Müller joined the duo of ball and Goalkeeper and made it a trio!

Situations that looked defensive certainties could never be considered so when he was playing. He had the character and determination to follow up on what others, less committed, would consider 'lost causes'. Müller was a 'defence disturber' who forced defences to make mistakes on which he preyed. He was a football 'dog', snapping and chasing at the heels of opponents giving them no time to play.

Goals to him were not artistically moulded. Goals to him meant the 'ball over the goal line'! If at the same time he and several other defenders also finished in the net, so what – a goal is a goal!

Müller had an exceptional scoring record for club and country. In the classy atmosphere of German football, he partnered such greats as Beckenbauer and Breitner. He was admired for mental strength and his persistence. He was truly a 'cutting-edge' for the German football machine during their successful World Cup winning years.

Müller made the best out of a limited playing ability. But he forged his success on determination and being prepared to go that extra little bit further than others. Müller's belief was, like so many goalscorers, 'you keep going to the shop to buy a ticket to have a chance of winning the big prize'. For him the shop was the crowded goal area and his prize was goals: lots and lots of them.

Player to Watch: Didier Drogba, Chelsea, Ivory Coast

The parts of the football world that are still economically poor are still producing players of exceptional talent. Drogba is a fine example of poverty producing players.

From crowded street games to the international stage, Drogba, has been a clear example for all to see of the playing qualities each stage of his development has brought to his game.

His early days at Chelsea began with indifferent performances as he came to terms with the rush and tough style of the English game. Goals were few and far between and spectators were impatient with his performances.

However, his mental strength and his determination to succeed sustained him and gradually he has improved his game to such an extent he now is elevated to 'super-status' amongst football followers at Chelsea and around the football globe.

His speedy athleticism combined with skill makes him a fearful competitor. He forces defenders to be at the very top of their game through his energy, skill and goal scoring ability. Like all outstanding goalscorers, he has a scoring instinct that sees him prepared to take chances others would not consider. He scores with either foot from all distances and is powerful in the air.

For both club and country he is a vital part of their football future. He is modern scorer with a high individual playing pedigree, produced, in the streets to be ultimately seen in stadiums.

CHAPTER 12

HEADING - THE FOOTBALL PERFECTIONISTS 'BLIND SPOT'

Football perfectionists, when referring to playing style tend to overlook the importance of Heading in the game.

The Laws of Association Football allow the ball to be headed and accordingly, this skill should take an important role in the playing 'repertoires' of both players and teams.

Whenever the ball can be moved quickly and effectively along the ground, every effort should be made to do so, but sometimes in a game, it may be better to play the ball in the air, heading then becomes a vital skill in both the attacking and defensive phases of the game.

The art of heading is a skill that must be learned from junior level (from about 11 years of age in my opinion). It should be carefully introduced and monitored by coaches as accidents or incorrect use of the head can produce a dislike for heading in young players. It is also important to note that the ball should be lightweight, with deliveries for heading made over short distances and at slow speed in the early stages.

Interceptions during early practice by opponents should be made with the open hand, not with the head! Later, as players become more accustomed to aerial challenge, they can compete for the ball in the air using their heads.

In the majority of circumstances heading is another form of passing the ball. The use of the head must follow the same standards as all other passing methods. However, when there is a need to clear the ball with the head when under defensive pressure, the ball should be sent high, wide and decisively away from danger.

The various methods of heading the ball is something I do not intend to focus on in this book. My aim in this chapter is to illustrate the use of heading as an alternative option in the game.

Whenever possible good players use their heading skills in a positive way to find a colleague with the ball or to put the ball into the opponents' goal. At times in our domestic game, players tend to use their head as a first option even when the ball could be controlled. This tendency often creates ball loss in situations in which possession could have been retained. Even in defending the use of the head should be used to clear to a colleague if possible. However, the decision to pass or clear danger must be quickly assessed in these rear areas as mistakes may not be easily or quickly rectified.

The ability to dominate in the air in rear defensive areas lessens the responsibility on goalkeepers to venture too far from their goal to catch or punch the ball.

Size is important in football. I'm not disputing the quality of the smaller player who is quick, strong and skillful; there is room for quality in any team. However, there are positions in a team that require height and aerial power. Unfortunately, too often these positions and roles have been accepted by our game as areas that need less all-round skillful players. Why should so many taller player with good heading ability be excused for having poor skills elsewhere? Brazil produce the 'total package' for these positions, if they can, so should we!

Whether at the back, in mid-field or in forward attacking positions, aerial quality must be combined with all other skills needed in the game.

In mid-field, it is fine to have neat and industrious players, but lack of aerial power in this central area can prove a debilitating feature in team performance if opposing teams dominate in aerial duels. Too often in cases where one team excels in the air in mid-field the ball can be directed towards their forward players positioned close to the opposition's last line of defence.

Initiative in football is vital – first gaining it, then retaining it. Teams who fail to dominate in the air in both mid-field and at the back have great difficulty achieving the initiative in a game and retaining it – therefore winning becomes less likely.
Likewise, heading power in forward, attacking positions is crucial for consistent success. In conjunction with other skills, heading quality provides alternative attacking options. Whether the head is used to pass the ball to a better-placed player or is 'passed' or 'powered' into the opposition's goal, the use of aerial quality can be the third essential ingredient in the 'winning cocktail'

1. Individual skills
2. Combined team play
3. Aerial power.

Crossing is one of the most important features in goal scoring. Crossing provides more goal scoring chances than all other types of play or delivery. Goal chances can come from high crosses towards the back of the goal; crosses to the centre of the goal; or near-post crosses. Crosses from deeper areas from the goal (diagonal crosses) are also important to supply headers for 'knock-downs' to supporting players or headers at goal.

In all of the above crossing situations, movement by attacking players combined with the accuracy of crossing skills can be a devastating prelude to a goal, but the best movement and most accurate of crosses will not bring success unless aerial power and determination is also available.

The significance of re-starts (free-kicks; corners; throw-ins) has become more obvious in today's game. Non-creative outfield play is providing less goal scoring opportunities and this has thrown more and more emphasis on to heading in both attacking and defending at re-start situations. Teams lacking size and power in the air become vulnerable at the back and unsuccessful in attack; in so doing they reduce their playing options and with that, their chances of winning.

Let me take this chance to make myself absolutely clear; I'm not a member of the 'Direct Play' brigade. The philosophy of direct football is too simplistic and presents mediocrity as a target of achievement in my opinion. Heading is a skill. An important one, but it should not override a higher conception of the game by both individuals or the teams in which they play. 'Total football quality must include heading ability alongside all the other skills of the game if we are to develop young players capable of playing and winning regularly at the top of world football.

PLAYERS TO WATCH

Defence: Ayala – Vaencia /Argentina

I've used Ayala, because he actually does not conform to the point I have stressed about the importance of size. Ayala, has been at the very top of the game at both club and international levels for well over a decade. He is an outstanding header of the ball. Although he is relatively small in comparison to most central defenders, he achieves aerial supremacy in defending and attacking situations through a combination of excellent timing and jumping power.

Due to his smaller physical size, Ayala is unlike most of his contemporaries, he is recognised for his all-round playing quality and is most comfortable with the ball at his feet. Aligned with his skills on the ground and in the air, his speed and tactical awareness has made him a legend in countries in Europe and South America.

Ayala, is a wonderful example of small not necessarily meaning failure. But he has been fortunate to have a strong physique to provide the surge to his game he uses so athletically.

Mid-Field: Vieira – Juventus/France

Vieira, is a fine example of all-round football quality. During his time at Arsenal F.C. where he matured into a world-class player, he displayed the 'Total Football' qualities so important in a player performing in a mid-field role at the top of the game.

Vieira was a leader, not just a captain of the team but an inspirational talent that dominated the football scene wherever he played.

He had a large physique and used it most effectively in both attack and defence. Vieira. was dynamic in all parts of the field. His heading power was dominant when defending and attacking.

A truly fine player, capable, like so many of the greats of the game – able to play in any position and make an impressive impact.

Attack: Drogba – Chelsea

Drogba, is a classic example of football athleticism combined with skill. Whether in forward or defensive positions he is comfortable in all types of situations. Most coaches call attacking players back to defend at re-start situations with some apprehension, for they fear a change in positional duty can often lead to a loss in concentration from a player. Drogba, defends like he attacks – with enthusiasm, power and concentration.

Heading is just one of Drogba's skillful assets, but it is a powerful influence in his performances as well as his team. His stature, combined with his speed, skills and game understanding make him a handful for all opposing teams.

Chelsea, have utilised Drogba's heading as well as his other skills are used to best effect. Players support him eagerly, for they have become confident in his ability to find them with head or feet. His goal scoring record speaks for itself, for with both head and feet he is a regular 'hitter of the net'.

Drogba, is a fine example of a physical footballer. A secure asset when defending; a superb winner when attacking.

CHAPTER 13

GOALKEEPERS, THE DEEPEST SWEEPERS

Goalkeeping is a specialised branch of football. In the past, goalkeepers have been more reminiscent of both handball or basketball players – their handling of the ball, has been the dominating feature of their game. Not so today. Goalkeepers use their feet a great deal more in today's game and must show the same level of competence as outfield players.

The changes in the laws governing 'The Back Pass', to goalkeepers has dramatically changed the role and scope of goalkeeping in football today. No longer allowed to handle passes back to them from foot or throw-ins, goalkeepers have to use their feet more.

It is a common sight in the game to see goalkeepers placed under pressure due to their limited kicking skills. Too many make costly errors or fail to provide positive play from their deep position. A great many goalkeepers are one-footed and are uncomfortable when the ball is at their 'wrong' foot. Being closed-down and forced to play the ball with their weaker foot, often causes embarrassment for goalkeepers resulting in costly mistakes.

Skill on the ball has become an absolute necessity if goalkeepers are to reach the highest standard. Present day goalkeepers are expected to accept a more constructive role in overall team play. 'Stopping' the ball is no longer enough; goalkeepers must also be equally competent at 'starting and re directing' attacking play from the back of their team.

The new laws on the pass back increased long forward kicking by goalkeepers. The laws may have speeded the game up, but it decreased thrown deliveries from goalkeepers. What has resulted is that goalkeepers have become more likely to kick the ball long often out of play or perpetuate direct play methods. Too often team possession is lost through goalkeeper's eagerness to clear the ball up field.

In common with their back defenders, who are equally uncomfortable on the ball, the long ball forward has emerged as the most likely attacking tactic to be used by most teams in our game. This form of long-range frontal assault is the easy option for uncertain and low-skilled players at the back. This form of delivery has created a game style based on aerial duels between competing defenders and forwards, with surrounding players becoming 'scavenging hyenas' picking up the bits and pieces that fall in their direction.

There is far more opportunity to play controlled football from back positions than is seen in our game at present. Pressurising of defenders is not always possible by the opposition. When the opportunity occurs or is created to play with more subtlety from back area, all players, including the goalkeeper must be capable and confident to do so.

The over emphasis on long, forward passing places ball possession at risk, often without need. Better understanding of developing attacking play from deep must become a common feature on our practice and playing grounds.

Goalkeepers must expect to take a much more active role in establishing and retaining good ball possession for their teams. From their deep, supportive positions behind their team-mates, goalkeepers must be prepared to receive the ball from one side of the field, and using their feet, transfer it quickly and accurately to the other side of the field.

Goalkeepers are positioned perfectly in their 'back play-round area' and even from the 'defending play-round area' to play a leading part in the construction of their team's initial attacking preparation.

Two-footed goalkeepers are becoming as important as two-footed out-field players. Being closed-down and forced onto a weaker side must not be a fault that opposing teams can exploit. Forcing goalkeepers to kick the ball into block A of the nearest stand should only be an option of last resort for goalkeepers – not first thought!

Goalkeepers must use the time and space they so often have more effectively. They must be fully aware of the attacking and possession possibilities that are available to them in conjunction with their back players. Goalkeepers must appreciate that in most circumstances, they are the 'spare player'. Accordingly, goalkeepers must have skills with their feet as with their hands. To acquire these skills and tactical awareness, goalkeepers should not be isolated on training grounds, but integrated more with the work of outfield players.

As I have stated throughout this book, bravery to change, adapt, take in new information is required within our game. The importance of goalkeepers as 'the deepest sweeper' must be recognised and acted upon by coaches for all ages. Surely, to add another 'attacking player' and more attacking options to teams is what coaches should be investigating – goalkeepers fit the bill.

Coaching must improve its goalkeeping programmes. Coaches must be encouraged to work with goalkeepers and increase the responsibilities on the goalkeeper when on the ball or in a supportive position. Goalkeepers must be able to 'split' opposing players and with the ball at their feet play passes like an outfield player.

Goalkeepers must be prepared to 'overload' to add their presence in preparation for attacking play from the back.

The bravery is – how far will coaches allow 'keepers to move forward to assist their back players to develop attacking play from deep?

How is the goalkeeper's move from goal to be covered should a mistake occur? What alternatives are available if attacking play from the back is restricted by fast closing down of opponents?

Do the advantages of involving goalkeepers more frequently in attacking play outdo the disadvantages?

All of these questions need brave answers. Are we to retain the old image of the game of 10 outfield versus 10 outfield, or can the goalkeepers be the added dimension so necessary for improved team play and better back possession?

The game needs astute bravery, not stupid recklessness. The work and increased responsibility on goalkeepers needs to find the right balance. Goalkeepers are the 'deepest sweepers'; with all that time and space they must be used far more as 'starters' of attacking play.

If the back can provide – the front will deliver!

Player to Watch: Edwin Van Der Sar, Holland

Ajax FC, are renowned for the clever and thoughtful footballer's they produce and the way they play the game. Their style of play has been exciting to watch and successful both domestically and internationally.

Their brand of football is built upon the skillful qualities of individuals who combine those skills into a highly effective game/style. There are a host of international stars who have come through the Ajax development programme, but a special place of honour must be set aside for, Van Der Sar, a goalkeeper who reflects their football doctrine, for he was their 'deepest sweeper'.

Van Der Sar, is a great goalkeeper. He has all the normal qualities expected of a top-class player in this position; but he has more; he is also skillful with the ball at his feet. This extra bonus elevates him above all other goalkeepers in my opinion. He has found no problem coping with the new back-pass rule and has been an important part of all the teams for whom he has played.

Attacking play from deep is something that needs to be recognised as quickly as possible; started with care; nurtured with patience; exploited with speed. Van Der Sar, from his goalkeeping position has the ability to provide all the requirements mentioned.

He is outstanding in his ability to support his defenders, making himself available for them should they become pressurised by opponents. With the ball at his feet he is quite capable of launching, long forward passes with either left or right foot, but usually he demands more of himself and provides shorter passes to his back or mid-field team-mates. He is also capable of taking the ball forward himself between opposing players before passing the ball. Van Der Sar is the sweeper with 'gloves on'; a goalkeeper who is also a footballer.

Good ball possession has always been a cornerstone of his goalkeeping performances. At all the clubs he has played for he has provided them with a platform from which to develop controlled attacking play from the back. Because of this, all players through the teams who have had Van Der Sar as their goalkeeper have been able to produce exciting game styles in which all players have been able to display their full potential.

Coaching must realise the true importance of goalkeepers within the whole framework of team play. The increased tactical options available by using the goalkeeper more freely needs careful consideration. Most certainly, better 'government' of the ball from back to front is possible when the goalkeeper is more skillful.

It must be an accepted fact in the game that goalkeepers should play a more vital supportive part in attacking play, for if the back can't, the front won't!

CHAPTER

DEFENDING - THE FOUNDATION OF COMPETITIVE SUCCESS

'Winning does not really matter as long as you win'
Vinnie Jones

Coach A: 'We played some really great football today.'
Coach B: 'Oh, how did you get on?'
Coach A: 'We lost 3-4.'
Coach B: 'Oh, you lost.'

Let's not beat about the bush and be honest: competitive football at all levels is about winning! It may not mean quite so much at junior levels to lose, but it should still hurt!

The attempt to take the issues of winning and losing from the playing equation has not proved successful for both the sport or for the youngsters playing it. How can you tell any player not to want to win !

Don't think I'm one of those people who regard just winning as the pinnacle of performance. No, winning should occur through quality play. The problem we face here in this country, is the amount of competitive play without a quality teaching and learning structure to support it. Winning here is more about exiting successfully from a fierce battle, than overcoming the opposition with a combination of skill, athleticism and game understanding.

As described in the conversation between the two coaches, it means little to play well and lose. We all want to play attractive, free-flowing football, but to be able to play it and win needs quality coaching throughout the whole development process or all you get is honest effort as a result.

Winning creates confidence; losing brings anxiety. You only lose football matches if the opposition score more goals than you do, therefore, you must make sure that they don't score against you; in a 'nutshell' you've got to defend well.

I don't intend to go deeply into all, aspects of defending, but simply address some areas concerning defending that I feel are in need of more attention.

As the chapter heading states, defending is the foundation of competitive success. In all competitive team sports it is necessary to overcome the opposition and achieve attacking initiative over them. Attacking initiative is the vital ingredient towards successful results. Good defending is also the start of attacking play. Unless the ball is regained from the opposition you can't start to attack yourself !

Solidity when defending throughout the whole team is an absolute necessity; gaps means goals against! From the front to the goalkeeper, all players must know their roles in the defensive structure of the team, with all of them prepared to defend when required to do so – the 'temperamental star' who switches off once he is required to defend is often more of a liability than an asset. There is no reason why playing quality should not include a responsible defensive attitude as well!

All successful teams are capable of defending from the front. The initial 'first defensive barrier' is formed by players more usually associated with attacking not defending. If these forward players apply themselves properly to the defensive job they can create a formidable 'barrier' to the opposition a considerable distance from their goal. In so doing, they can supply their team-mates in deeper playing roles with visual information that can assist these players to make decisions on their marking and covering positions.

The ability of front players to defend with some expertise can also mean that the ball can be regained close to the opposition's goal with all the obvious benefits. But should early repossession not be possible delay must be the defensive objective. The decisions on whether to attempt early ball repossession or retreat to delay the opposition are extremely important. Allowing the opposition too much of the ball too often can affect your own initiative in the game; whilst defending in a disorderly and ill-timed fashion can leave gaps for opponents to exploit. Defending is a whole team effort built on a network of individuals, Being attack-minded when your team is required to defend is not a satisfactory response!

Guiding attacking play into less dangerous areas often begins at the front and is supported at the back. The question of which way to send opposing attacking players inside or outside, is a heated subject. Some prefer inside, some outside, each has a plus and minus. My own preference in most cases was to direct play wide unless reasons dictated otherwise, for at worst my defenders had to deal with a cross and not several other options available to attackers should they come inside with the ball.

Another significant change in defensive play has been the wide-spread use of a 'flat' back defensive line of players. This defensive strategy was actually created to assist attacking play by positioning full-backs in a more advanced position to (a) be closer to opposing flank players, and (b) to be in a more advanced position to support their own team's attacking play down the flanks.

I must admit, I am not a supporter of 'flat' defensive play. I believe too many chances on goal are occurring through malfunctioning of this defensive strategy. This method of defending, especially under the new offside laws which have been imposed, has created too much uncertainty too close to goal for my liking. Decisions on offside are too finely balanced and can be easily mis-applied by players or mis-read by officials. I also have a strong dislike of seeing one pass beat a 'flat' line of players when a normal balanced defence would have had no difficulty dealing with such situations.

In a 'nutshell', defending, using a 'flat' line at the back, has become too risky, I am not in the risk business and prefer the cover from a 'balanced' defensive covering system as my insurance !

Defensive marking at crossing situations is something that playing on the half-turn is all about. So often, defenders positioning at crosses is incorrect, not allowing them to see both the play around them or make quick movements back or forward as the attackers they are marking make their runs.

Good defenders must always be first to the ball. Coming second can mean a goal against and a match lost.

One of my pet complaints in the game today is the marking at re-starts eg central and wide free-kicks around the penalty area. The marking against both of these types of free-kick retains the defensive strategies of the past in my opinion.

The change in the materials of the ball and its tendency to move more in the air than older types did; the improvement in footwear that increases touch and encourages players to use more 'spin' on the ball to bend in flight; plus the cult of 'Beckhamism', in following his 'dead-ball' techniques has made defending against free-kicks near to goal an increasing problem.

The defending against both of these types of free-kicks continues to see the adoption of the set-up that requires space to be left between the deepest defender and the goalkeeper. This space is supposed to give the 'keeper a better view of the ball, but it is now a space that is being exploited too often by cunning delivery of the ball into it, forcing defenders to defend whist running back towards their own goal.

The central free-kick is regularly being taken to go over/under and around defensive walls leaving the goalkeeper little chance of making a save.

The wide, inswinging free-kicks also are being taken with more quality than in the past, with once again the ball being delivered into the space between deepest defenders and the goalkeeper with alarming results for defences.

Neither of the present defensive methods is proving satisfactory and more thought must go into making changes to marking at these situations.

Whatever defensive system that is the preference of the coach, results will be its test; goals against and loss equals failure; 'clean sheets' and victories means – everything !

CHAPTER

SOME
TACTICAL
THOUGHTS

So many of the games in this country remind me of the senseless tactics employed in the First World War. 'Trench warfare' tactics undertaken across the whole of the Western Front used a ponderous 'hit-for-hit' mentality. Both military forces were unable to find ways of overcoming the other and stagnation interspersed with deathly frontal attacks by both sides continued almost to the end of the conflict. Was this attritional military approach too different from the; straight-lined, straight running, straight passing tactics we see so frequently at all levels of our national game? I don't think so.

Football is a game allowing a full range of movement. To assist in the movement of play in both attacking and defensive situations, teams are required to use tactical shapes. The decisions on which shape is selected depends on many circumstances; a coach may prefer using a particular system; another may copy the system of a different team because of their success; another selects a way of playing that suits the playing ability of the players at his disposal. Irrespective of the reasons for, or type of team shape, all teams play using a shape of one sort or another.

The preferred team shape used extensively throughout the UK follows a 'dreary', predictable pattern – 4-4-2. There are occasional adaptations, but this is a rare occurrence – from junior games to senior international football we are 'hooked' on 4-4-2.

Tactical variations to change team shapes or playing styles is indeed a rarity. Fixed, straight lines of players are hardly ever 're-designed' to achieve tactical dominance, surprise or improve team combination and movement. Like the tactics of 1914-18, a direct frontal approach is preferred from our 'brave and bloodied' players instead of a more subtle use of staggered deployment and fast positional interchange to produce skillful football.

This 'blind' obedience towards structured play is most noticeable when substitutions are made during a game. Rarely are changes to playing personnel made to alter team shape or playing method. Other than for injury or red-card avoidance, substitutions are made to; withdraw a poorly performing player or to inject a new 'soldier 'into the 'battle' to 'beef it up' (usually meaning sticking a big 'un up front, hitting him on the head with the ball and fighting like dogs for the proceeds !

Generally, substitutions follow a like-for-like positional exchange allowing the 'attritional conflict' to continue unabated. A newly inserted 'Fred Bloggs' is expected to imitate perfectly the 'qualities' of the rejected 'Jim Smith'. I am often forced to ask myself why 'Fred Bloggs' was not selected before 'Jim Smith', their contributions to the 'battle' being so alike provides no added problems for the opposition other than simply introducing 'fresh-legged, cattle fodder' to the fray!

As I have tried to emphasise throughout this book, the alarming lack of individual skills at all levels of our game has demanded that a simplistic game-style is played, whereas the more skillful players available to the game, the more expansive the tactics and game-style can be.

Ball possession by individuals and by teams requires skillful play. Presently it is one of the least effective areas of our game. It never surprises me to hear all our national coaches and media complain that squads for decades have failed in one competition after another because the teams 'gave the ball away too easily'. Skill deficiency is at the heart of the problem. How can players suddenly become 'ball-conscious' when for years they have been forced, through poor teaching, to play a form of football that does not emphasise the importance of ball possession or to develop the skills to make it happen?

Skill deficiency is the centre-point for the ring of negative 'waves' that have spread out into all areas of our game. In the tactical consideration of ball possession by our teams, most of our problems are caused by 'un-connected' team formations. The need for rigid compliance to 'structured, comfortable, positional occupation' by players (uncomfortable outside their own 'cage') has meant a lack of skillful players capable of 'living' in the ' no-mans land' between the attritional lines of play. This lack of 'half-positional' playing quality, has increased the need to play from back-to-front using long passes irrespective of other playing opportunities that are often possible. This over-use of direct play methods and its lack of certainty in ball possession creates problems with linkage and hinders combined team movements. The flow of attacking football is too erratic and any goal-chances that do occur tend to come from mistakes being forced onto opponents rather than from clever team play.

Tactical improvement in attacking play needed here in the UK is immense. Basically, we only use one way to start off our attacking play – knock it long, challenge (usually in the air up front), chase and fight for 'knock-downs'. I am not suggesting that playing off the results of a long forward pass is wrong, but it shouldn't be a singular weapon in our football arsenal. Better possession based on more options, improved ball delivery and closer support, must go side-by-side with the long forward pass.

Unless (1) ball delivery to players is careful; (2) ball reception is assured; (3) linkage is quickly available, tactical considerations are impossible to apply. All of these three categories are poor in our game. It isn't surprising then that we have been unable to achieve any real consistency in our play or our results at all international levels. Don't tell me our top clubs do well in European competitions, they're full of foreign talent that in most cases have not become infected with the British disease of what I term 'ball-sacrificeity'.

Most of our goals are scored as a result of a crossing situation. What is not generally understood by most inside the game as well as press and public on the outside, is the obvious but nevertheless overlooked point that a cross is a pass!

Yes, passes to provide goal scoring chances! Being a pass, it should be delivered with all the care and thought as any other pass. Too often our game tolerates poor ball delivery from crosses without complaint. Well, it's only a cross seems to be the general attitude. Good crossers of the ball are the 'kings of assists' and are essential parts to any successful team. Poor crossers who deliver without looking to see where or who to cross to; deliver from too deep from goal; hit opposing defenders positioned in the front of the goal area with the ball; or cross in a haphazard fashion without picking out players accurately, are a pain in the 'butt', for their wasteful use of the ball from these important areas is inexcusable.

Crossing is the end-product of flank play and these 'passes' should be delivered with quality, not just wasteful quantity.

CHAPTER

16

MIXING THE
GAME-STYLES

Being able to mould a mixture of individual talent into a successful team is what good coaching is all about at senior levels.

Not every coach can be a winner of trophies at a season's end, but every coach can earn accolades for their effort to produce teams prepared to play with style and cleverness.

Imaginative coaching methods, produces imaginative players, who will play imaginative football!

Football is a clever game. It is immensely flexible in both shape and content, thereby allowing a multitude of ideas to be tried. Because of the playing possibilities the game allows, automatons should have no place in it! The bravery to accept the challenge to achieve excellence must be applauded. Playing methods pandering to low skill levels must be short-term necessities until our skills and understanding have improved. Skill, in all its forms, is the bedrock of the game. This important concept must never be forgotten. Any attempts to impose long-term, over-simplistic methods on the game must be fiercely rejected.

It is vitally important that high levels of individual skill should be available from all positions – the more the skills available; the more the playing options become available throughout the team!

All great teams display a balanced tactical mix within their playing styles for attacking and defending situations. The selection of a mixed game-style provides the chance to play long or short according to the circumstances at the time. The argument over the respective merit of long or short passing game styles is a futile exercise, for neither is satisfactory if used independently and constantly.

Good teams make better decisions than poor ones. Young talent must be developed to play different game- styles with differing positional roles to increase their understanding and all around playing quality.

It should be clearly understood that to restrict children the opportunity of acquiring high levels of individual skill and understanding for the game is indefensible on the part of those who propose to teach it. Coaches, especially those developing young players, must never produce players to perform a 'robotic' playing style purely to satisfy their own ego for success. To be part of the 'win-at-all-cost' brigade is to be guilty of child neglect and abuse!

For too long, results not playing quality, has dominated our development structure. Fear of failure has led coaching to limit performance to reduce mistakes. A direct playing style fitted the need completely.

Long, forward passes, followed by the whole team moving quickly up field in order to 'squeeze' the opposition deep into their own half, has been a regular sight at all playing levels in our country. 'Route-one' football, as it has been described, is the simplified, repetitive game style that requires more effort than skill to play it.

Our development structure has weaned our young talent to provide easy options only. The outcome has been a frightening loss of quality from our game and winning has dominated learning objectives.

Pressure football, with the emphasis on quick territorial gain is more likely to achieve success from forced effort than creative cleverness; nevertheless, it should be a part of every good team's playing style. The use of direct play methods for the right reasons can give a team a strong psychological advantage over their opponents. It clears pressure near their own goal and transfers that pressure to the opponents's goal.

Field Marshal Montgomery, emphasised in his Battle Doctrine; 'Fight on ground of your own choice: Seize the initiative in the battle and keep it'.

How right he was, for using direct play methods in a calculated way, a team 'earns the right' to play more sophisticated football from the time, space and territorial advantage that this form of playing style can achieve. Unfortunately, for our game there has been a disastrous lack of effort by coaches to teach this next phase!

Direct play 'pushes the door ajar', but there are insufficient coaches and players capable of opening the door completely! We have become satisfied with the 'lazy-man's way of playing' the sledgehammer is retained where slinky skills are required!

Liverpool, in their glory years of the late 1980s and early '90s, provided the clearest and most balanced mixture of game styles. They combined the forceful aspects of the British game to provide the time/space to inject a cultured short passing style into their game normally only seen abroad.

Gradually a few more clubs have followed Liverpool's mixed style example, but all have leaned heavily on the influence of foreign stars to provide the skills.

Playing in a direct manner does create space on the football field; space becomes available at the back of the attacking team as they 'squeeze' forward. This space has not been used satisfactorily as a 'launching pad' to develop more controlled and clever football from.

Our history of player development has shown a disregard for change in the production of defensive players. 'Sound, rather than skillful' best describes the generations of back players supplied to our game. Because of this, the enormous attacking possibilities that could emanate from defensive areas of the field have largely been ignored.

Having skillful players in defensive positions, would improve playing flexibility and create a better, mixed and balanced style of play to our game. Field Marshal Montgomery, when discussing battle tactics said 'train your soldiers properly for the job they are to do: carefully select the ground on which to engage the enemy; disrupt the enemy with a decisive 'punch' (direct play) to achieve the initiative in the battle; never lose the initiative (ball possession); keep the army balanced at all times (rotation); place reserve formation's behind the main thrust (half positions) to quickly exploit attacking advantage, or defend any enemy counter-attack; every attacking force must contain soldiers with mixed military ability (to attack or defend with skill); should an attack stall, force must be re-directed to less strongly held position's (play-rounds).'

Montgomery could have been a football coach discussing his game plan. The principles of warfare sit comfortably alongside the principles of Association Football.

Morale and spirit are necessary ingredients in the composition of a good team. Generals as well as football coaches respect the importance of effort and attitude amongst their 'troops'. But skill and understanding must form the sound base on which all the supplementary qualities so necessary for success, can be set.

Defending is a skill. Too often British defenders have displayed the 'bull-dog' spirit in excess of guile and adaptation. The lack of high quality coaches has meant a serious downturn in the adaptability of defenders in this country, and defending as an individual has become a lost art!

The over-emphasis of 'pressure-play' tactics requiring fast defensive closing down methods by a whole team, is extremely hard to sustain, especially when so much effort is also expended in producing fast attacking play. Pressure-play, as a defensive ploy is useful when correctly used. If over-done, it can be both physically exhausting and tactically naive.

The when and how to use pressure-play tactics both offensively and defensively, and properly, mixed with other methods of attack and defence, must be taught more readily in the future. If we require fast, agile, intelligent, strong, skillful, offensive players, we must also produce players with similar qualities to defend against them! It means a break from conventional and historical beliefs about individual and group defensive qualities. Being only able to provide combative ability to the game is no longer enough to fulfill the larger demands of the game. The 'bulk over brains' mentality must disappear quickly if we are to improve our football standards.

The success of all winning teams is built on good defence. Playing nice football and losing will not be tolerated at any level for too long. Individual players make up the whole of a team. One weak link can penalise the whole team structure. Good defenders are not embarrassed marking 1v1. Likewise good defenders should be able to participate in attacking play with the same lack of embarrassment.

As mentioned earlier in this book 'overloading' of all parts of a team, whether from outflanking or inner-overloading situations is vital. The 'attacking-defender' and the 'defensive-attacker' must exist freely within a game-style that favors flexible movement above solid confrontational methods.

Coaches and their players must show bravery to practice examples of 'total football' and then, allow it to be played!

How long must it be before we see British players in British teams mixing their game with a combination of: British zest with foreign best!

CHAPTER 17 CONCLUSIONS

I hope the reader will have found this book interesting and informative.

Each chapter has controversial points that I hope will be considered carefully. I hope it also opens discussions on the importance of developing a national game/style.

I have attempted to illustrate what I believe to be weaknesses on both the practical and organisational sides of the game in this country. These deficiencies have eventually led to a disturbing crisis in our game; where is the quality young talent for the future? Other countries need to be aware similar problems do not occur in their football!

In this final chapter, I will expand on the reasons for the demise in our playing quality and offer some ideas to improve our development structure for the future. Let's start at the very beginning: Junior Football. What a shambolic, disgraceful mess! I have been a severe and continuous critic of our 'patchwork', disorganised approach at this, the foundation level of our game.

From it inception, I believe the ESFA have been a major contributing factor leading towards the present demise of homebred football talent. Fed by players, self- developed on the streets of the nation, arguably the ESFA were, nonetheless, happy to organise a national structure in which these youngsters played competitive matches. Little thought was given to player instruction and development.
Young players, with skill, desire, athleticism, but little football knowledge progressed through school football, some to the upper levels of the game. Professional clubs were similarly unconcerned about the subject of player development – 'There's plenty more out there' was their attitude. But as street football 'died' the positive effect it had on practice whilst playing went unappreciated by both academics and professional football here.

It wasn't until the professional game suddenly realised that the stream of talent was drying up, that provoked them through The FA to demand coaching time with young players. This request was fiercely objected to by the ESFA and although inadequate compromises were implemented, football development remained firmly in the hands of the Schools' Associations – who had no real development programme!.

After much in-fighting between The FA and ESFA the result was that pro clubs were allowed to create a national coaching school at Lilleshall and Centres of Excellence or Academies for the more talented youngsters, whilst the rest of football's aspiring youngsters were left in the hands of well-intentioned, but in terms of coaching, football ignorant parents.

Irrespective of who had control over the development time for young players, the content and quality use of that time remains, on the whole, unsatisfactory. Schools' football had virtually ignored development needs; the FA introduced poor coaching into the equation.

For all the expense incurred by The FA from their Lilleshall experiment the increase in their international development programme – changes to their coaching programmes – plus numerous other false starts, no satisfactory progress in playing standards has occurred.

The FA coaching and development schemes, over many decades have failed to produce quality players in sufficient numbers; yet they continue to preach a message that has a long history of under-achievement. There is a feeling that coach education is... in a mess! In today's world footballer's are generally expected to follow progressive coaching programmes. These programmes must contain top quality, realistic work; they must be delivered to both aspiring coaches and players by top quality football educators – neither of these factors exist! It seems to me, our football educators are more comfortable in front of a computer in a classroom, than in front of a group of players on a football field! Learning football is no different than learning about other subjects. The learner must develop through the subject stage by stage; you don't teach algebraic equations before lessons on addition and subtraction etc. The FA must introduce the game through their learning programmes in far more subtle way. Children must practice what they're expected to play. More 'game associated' practice incorporating specially designed competitive games must be introduced into the development programmes. These practices and the games applied to them must lead young players gradually towards the bigger game.

What can be done? Well, it's going to take brave decisions and the combined effort from both government and from within the game itself to reverse the present serious situation.

The government must look seriously at the school day! It's time of start; it's time of finish; the contents of the curriculum. Obesity is a worrying new entry into the world of the young. Government must legislate quickly to provide more opportunities for the young to participate in sport.

The school day seems to me to be as much about child minding as child education in this country. A school day satisfies the working hours of parents; school holidays are historical throw-backs to farming. In most overseas countries, the school day starts and finishes earlier. Although sport is not usually a school subject, youngsters find more time is available to join clubs to follow their sporting interests.

Our foreign football opponents can spend far more hours each week developing their young players whereas, our school day is a restriction to practice time. Everything is either rushed or simply not attempted.

To overcome the lack of time available with their school or club, young players must do 'football homework' in order to increase their contacts on the ball. Young players must find ways to create individual practice time. As in the past in the streets, the use of rebound surfaces to play against must be sought by the youngsters or developed by industry for them to purchase. Rebound practice, whether played in isolation or with friends can be an important way for both skill and fitness to be attained.

Our youth players deserve every chance to succeed in our game. False horizons can no longer be endured and positive criticism must be allowed to clear away old-fashioned ideas and bring a 'classier act to town'.

We have always been a nation of 'fighters' prepared to go the distance. This inner-strength has seen us through some dark periods in our history. This competitive spirit; the will to win, is part of our social fabric. This winning desire must not be curtailed at any level in our game, but it must be introduced with more care and imagination throughout the development years.

Playing with skill, understanding, speed, and competitive spirit is the goal. Coaching our youth players and preparing them for the hostile world of professional football needs the subtle approach, not the bully!

Practice at all levels must be realistic. As young players develop space and time must be gradually withdrawn from them in their practice and playing situations. The ability to react to situations immediately must be nurtured from the earliest years and continued through youth into senior football.

Winning football matches is habit formed from winning in practice. What coaches at all levels must learn and incorporate into their practices is that, winning does not always have to be just the number of goals scored! Competitive winners must never be discouraged, but they must be taught to be 'total football' winners.

Our senior game is simply a clear reflection of the lack of development quality the players have experienced through their school and youth periods. So, how do they arrive at the top? Well, with a 'sprinkling of skill, a drop of understanding and an ocean of effort' is enough to see most of them through.

It often seems to me, that football clubs here don't need a manager or a coach, all they need is a motivator; someone who can 'whip-up' the passion in the players and send them kicking and fighting onto the field in a frenzy of effort to camouflage the lack of playing ability.

The position of manager at our clubs is still one of confused multiple roles. Does a manager here have control over the running of the club? Does he only control the business aspects of the club and delegate coaching responsibilities to others? Does he do a bit of both? Does he only work with the first team?

Successful businesses structure themselves efficiently in order to function effectively. Professional football, must also delegate more clearly to allow the game to operate successfully. Like the multiple confusion of management, so the multiple confusion of various 'interested parties' actively involved in running the game here, has led to so much disorganisation and disruption and lack of progress.

We must be extremely careful where our game and the structure surrounding it is going. Money is king! The pursuit of financial gain is thrusting our clubs into the hands of financial speculators, not football lovers on the whole.

Security of job and position no longer just follows the line of results, but are affected by stock-market figures and the whims of rich owners. The need to 'keep the books balanced' and if possible show a healthy profit often means cut-backs in the area of player development, with obvious repercussions into the senior game.

The senior game itself is about one thing: winning! To achieve this consistently, our top clubs look abroad for players, whilst those lower down are forced to play with the discards of bigger clubs or their own average products.

Winning without much ability on a regular basis is difficult. To stay in the race, managers and coaches are often forced to use restrictive game-style methods. Mistakes are not tolerated in your own half so the ball is 'hammered' down the other end of the field at every opportunity.

It might quite reasonably be asked; is the teaching of good football necessary or even desired? The fans say they want to see it, but won't allow it to be played – through fear of mistakes and losing. Managers and coaches don't impress it on their players, for fear of mistakes and losing; the players haven't been taught how to play it and rely on easy options for fear of mistakes and losing. So where do we go from here?

Honest discussion on the game's future followed by clear decisions must take place. Dishonest hype and pretence of quality must be shown for what it really is – LIES !

Unless we make radical changes to the government and practical issues relating to all areas of the game here we will descend from our present position (if honestly assessed) on the second tier of world football nations – to the third level. I have tried to carry the word brave forward throughout this book. I have mentioned how bravery can be demonstrated in various ways. It is only right that I should display bravery in my remarks about our game.

It only remains to say that our game requires brave decisions to be made by brave people for our game to be called, 'Football For The Brave'!